Contents

Keep trusting...

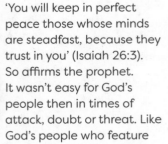

'You will keep in perfect peace those whose minds are steadfast, because they trust in you' (Isaiah 26:3). So affirms the prophet. It wasn't easy for God's people then in times of attack, doubt or threat. Like God's people who feature in this season's Bible readings (eg Elisha and Isaiah), today there is also suffering, mockery, persecution and failure of faith. Who knows what next year will bring? Yet there is this assurance of peace for those who, in spite of it all, keep their trust fixed in God and remain faithful to him.

Move on a few centuries to the time of the Gospels and we encounter the long-awaited Messiah, Jesus: bringer of good news. Our readings from Mark's Gospel allow us a disciple's-eye view. It wasn't as the disciples had expected, yet Jesus patiently teaches them (and us) the truth of what it means to follow him. Hope – as it was for God's ancient people and New Testament believers – can be difficult to hang on to. Habakkuk could have been overwhelmed by the disasters of his particular time; instead his example encourages us to assert our faith: 'Yet I will rejoice' (Habakkuk 3:18).

In spite of all that's wrong with our world today, let's continue to do that. And when words fail *us*, God provides *his* word through the psalms (see *Spotlight*).

Next year, keeping in mind comments of some readers, we are moving to shorter series, allowing more variety, but with the same level of engagement with the Bible and desire to meet with God as we read his Word. May God bless you this autumn. Keep trusting!

'Tricia and Emlyn Williams
Editors

loved it when the mission came because there wasn't much other excitement for a child in Sutton on Sea! Many of the families visiting for the mission stayed at the caravan park that my grandad owned, so they were part of my life from an early age.'

A gradual coming to faith

Her family weren't churchgoers, but Lottie's mother started taking her to the beach mission when she was still a toddler. 'The people were nice and she thought it would be safe and fun. We went every year and the people on the mission became like a second family. I really looked up to the volunteer team who ran it. When I was 6, I made myself a lanyard because they all wore them and I was desperate to be one of them!

'My faith mostly developed at the two weeks at beach mission each year.'

'When I got a bit older, I started thinking more deeply about why the team were the way they were and came to the conclusion that it was because of Jesus: because of their faith in him.

'Coming to faith myself was a gradual process. My faith mostly developed at the two weeks at beach mission each year. I didn't go to church the rest of the year, partly because my family didn't go anyway, and partly because I couldn't find a church that I felt at home in. So the beach mission was my spiritual home. The team really helped me

develop my understanding of faith, and I would say that I had become a Christian by the time I was 15.'

'I felt like I was falling ... but God would catch me'

However, Lottie does recall one pivotal moment. 'I really struggled in secondary school. One night I was in my bedroom, doing homework for subjects I hated, and I suddenly felt I had had enough. It felt like everything I was doing was for someone else, not for me, and I just couldn't do it any more. I felt like I was falling into a deep, dark pit...

'Then I looked up at a picture on my wall, of me and my beach mission group in 2005 when I was about 4 years old. I recalled the faith of the leaders and what they had taught me: that God won't give you a challenge that you can't get through, and that he's always with you. In that moment I realised that I wasn't alone. God was there. He was my safety net. He would always catch me and so I had no need to be afraid.'

Inspired to volunteer

Lottie says she was inspired by one of the beach mission team leaders who, like her, had no church background. 'It gave me hope that I too could be on the team and inspire other children without church connections. So when I turned 17, I volunteered. Unfortunately, the next summer we had to do the mission online because of COVID-19 and the national

lockdown! But I had fun helping to edit the videos for it, and at least we were able to meet, even if it wasn't in person.

'It was great to see around 150 adults and children sitting all across the beach.'

'Meanwhile, Sutton on Sea was eerily empty. When I went to the local shops, people I knew would ask me when the mission would be back. They honestly missed it. The mission team have an influence that extends beyond the beach because they genuinely care about the local people, not just those who come to the mission itself. The town is a low-income area and, because there's not much else for them to do, the mission is something local families can enjoy, even if they're not Christians. It doesn't cost them anything and it's a lot of fun.

'Thankfully, the following year we were back to having the beach mission in person again. It was great to see around 150 adults and children sitting all across the beach, with the adults taking part and doing all the actions to the songs as enthusiastically as the children!'

Finding confidence in sharing Jesus

Lottie helps to lead the Seahorses group for the duration of the beach mission. 'They're aged from 11 to 13. I know some people think it can be challenging looking after that age group, but I love being with them! They're very caring and make sure the quieter kids or those with special needs don't get left out.

'They're young enough to still want to play games and do craft, but they're also starting secondary school and getting to the stage of thinking for themselves and asking lots of questions. Sometimes I find those questions a bit challenging, having had no Christian upbringing, so I'm grateful to work with others on the team who know more about the Bible than I do. I can go to them with the harder questions, and I get to learn more about God too! Even though I'm starting from further back in terms of what I know than many of the other volunteers, I never feel like they judge me – they are always offering me encouragement. So my faith is growing, as is my confidence in sharing it.

'I love building relationships with the kids and helping them to explore faith, especially those without church backgrounds. Having no church background myself, I know that they can feel they are "different" from the other children, and I can understand where they're coming from. It's so rewarding when they ask questions about faith and genuinely want to know more. And it's so gratifying to know that I'm the one they trust to tell them about Jesus.'

A shorter version of this story first appeared in *Connecting You*, Scripture Union's free quarterly supporter magazine. If you'd like to receive copies of *Connecting You* and learn more of how God is moving in the hearts and lives of children and young people today, you can sign up on our website at su.org.uk/connectingyou.

THE RESTORATION STATION

RESTORATION STATION TOOLBOX

RESTORATION STATION LOGBOOK

Use with The Restoration Station holiday club.

Includes photocopiable resources and **FREE** extras online

A BRAND-NEW HOLIDAY CLUB RESOURCE FROM SCRIPTURE UNION

...liday club ...ew ideas, ...nce.

At *The Restoration Station* children will be introduced to Jesus as a restorer. Using key stories from John's Gospel, the children will discover how Jesus is the master craftsman who heals and restores.

GET THE RESTORATION STATION:
www.su.org.uk/therestorationstation

It's your turn now!

Have you ever taken over a job from someone else? In practice it often doesn't go very well! In theory, however, you will watch your predecessor doing the job, learn from him or her and build relationships with those you are going to work with. As you step into the role, you will seek to achieve a balance between continuity and making the role your own.

In 1 Kings 19 we read how God sends Elijah to anoint Elisha as his successor. Elisha accepts the invitation and goes with him, becoming his assistant. Between 1 Kings 19 and 2 Kings 2 there is a clearly intentional period of discipleship and mentoring: Elisha serves Elijah and assists him for a number of years. When Elijah is taken up to heaven, Elisha is ready to step straight into the role, acting and speaking with confidence. The other prophets watch Elisha pick up Elijah's cloak and very quickly recognise him as Elijah's successor, although some insist on going to look for Elijah. Elisha's spiritual authority is immediately displayed as he parts the Jordan (2 Kings 2:14) and then proceeds to perform the miracles we will read about over the next two weeks.

Though not a perfect parallel, there are lessons for us as disciples of our Master, Jesus. We walk with him and observe what he does, and also receive his Spirit so that we may continue to do his works (John 14:12-17; Acts 1:8).

About the writer
Alison Allen

After 14 years of being involved in mission in and from Romania, Alison returned to the UK in 2014 and now lives in Suffolk with her husband, two young children and three cats. Alison is currently working in the local Public Health department, whilst researching millennials in international mission for a PhD.

Psalm 112

Giving as worship

PREPARE
Sing a song of praise!

· ·

READ
Psalm 112

EXPLORE

One of the great things about the psalms is that they are so varied: you can always find one to express how you're feeling. Maybe this is the one for your mood today: life is great! Or maybe you are more in tune with the likes of Psalm 73, where the psalmist wonders why everything seems to go well for the wicked.

How do you feel about verses 2 and 3 right now? The psalmist admits that we are sometimes surrounded by darkness (v 4), but even then we can live in light and have no reason to fear (vs 7,8) if we trust in the Lord. We don't achieve this by trying hard or quashing our feelings, but rather by fearing the Lord and delighting in his commands (v 1). As we worship him and meditate on his greatness, the things that ordinarily would terrify us somehow seem less scary.

And that is what gives us the freedom to be generous (vs 5,9). It's easier to be generous with your money when you know that God will provide for you. Likewise, you can share freely your skills, your time and your home when you understand these things as gifts from God. Giving is worship, not because we often give as part of a church service, but because giving declares our dependence on God. That's why it makes people stop and wonder.

> Even in darkness light dawns for the upright, for those who are gracious and compassionate and righteous.
>
> **Psalm 112:4**

RESPOND
Is there some way in which God has blessed you that you could be sharing more freely with others?

· ·

Bible in a year: Isaiah 61,62; Hebrews 12

Two women; two miracles

PREPARE
Bring your requests and petitions to God (Philippians 4:6).

. . . .

READ
2 Kings 4:1–17

EXPLORE
One thing that ties these two tales together is that God loves family! These are two different stories of miracles with the same aim: a mother being able to hold her children. For the first woman, the family is broken by the tragedy of her husband's death and the fear of losing her children (v 1). The second woman has lived many years with the sadness and disappointment of not having children (v16b). Both find themselves in a place of emotional pain: one a sudden blow and the other a constant ache.

Each of us has a different story. Perhaps you had a happy childhood and then enjoy or enjoyed parenting. For many of us, though, 'family' is a word filled with pain. Our response to the pain can be different too: the first woman approached Elisha with her need, while the second tried to hide hers. God, however, saw and cared about both.

Elisha asks the first, 'How can I help you?' or, in another translation, 'What shall I do for you?' (v 2, NASB). He asks the second woman, 'What can be done for you?' (v 13). In the same way, Jesus asked a blind man, 'What do you want me to do for you?' (Mark 10:51). The Lord is always ready and willing to hear our requests.

> Elisha replied to her, 'How can I help you?'
> **2 Kings 4:2**

RESPOND
Thank God that he knows and cares about the needs in your family or your need of family. Pray for healing, restoration and provision in your own family.

. . . .

Bible in a year: Isaiah 63,64; Hebrews 13

2 Kings 4:18–37

Faith in his faithfulness

PREPARE

Think about the signs of the changing seasons around you. Which season do you find yourself in spiritually?

. . . .

READ

2 Kings 4:18–37

EXPLORE

For the Shunammite woman, her son was an incredible demonstration of God's love, generosity, power and faithfulness. We saw yesterday her reaction to Elisha's prophecy (4:16), which was not a refusal of the gift, but an expression of the fear that she would once again face disappointment. We don't know for sure, but she may well have prayed often for a child, and may now have given up praying because the years of unanswered prayer had caused so much pain. We do not know enough of her history to know whether she had never conceived, suffered miscarriages or watched her children die.

And now, this miracle child is taken away from her. As her fears of more pain are confirmed, her reaction to Elisha's prophecy is justified. The woman, however, refuses to accept that God would deceive her. Where many would have abandoned their faith, she runs

to the Lord's servant, and trusts that 'Everything is all right' (v 26). Elisha is not 'just' resurrecting a child here; he is fighting for God's reputation as faithful and true.

Whatever our circumstances, we can trust in the faithfulness of God. He has not promised that life will always go as we want, but he has promised that he loves us and is with us and one day there will be no more pain or sadness (Revelation 21:4).

'Did I ask you for a son, my lord? ... Didn't I tell you, "Don't raise my hopes"?'
2 Kings 4:28

RESPOND

If you are facing pain and discouragement, bring it to the Lord. If not, pray for those you know who face challenging times.

. . . .

Bible in a year: Isaiah 65,66; John 1

Miraculous provision

PREPARE

Pray for people serving the Lord in other lands.

READ

2 Kings 4:38–44

EXPLORE

In this passage we catch a glimpse of the day-to-day life of Elisha and other prophets. They were not unaffected by the world around them, having to forage for food (v 39) or depend on the goodwill of others (v 42) during a time of famine. As leader, Elisha appears to have carried responsibility for the upkeep of the entire group (vs 38,42), a fact underlined by the widow we saw in verse 1, who felt she had a claim on Elisha.

Once again in our days many struggle to make ends meet. God still can and still does provide for his people in miraculous ways. I have been privileged to hear many first-hand accounts of God's provision, both through miraculous multiplication and through well-timed gifts. It's scary not to know where your next meal is coming from; but it's awesome when God steps in, showing that he knows and cares about your need.

Some of us are called to be like the man from Baal Shalishah, donating some of our first fruits for the sustenance of others (v 42). And some of us are to be like Elisha (vs 42,43), receiving with thanks and then sharing what we are given, even though it doesn't look like there will be enough to go around (see also Mark 6:39–42).

'How can I set this before a hundred men?' his servant asked. But Elisha answered, 'Give it to the people to eat. For … the LORD says: "They will eat and have some left over."'

2 Kings 4:43

RESPOND

If you are in need, talk to the Lord about it. If you have plenty, consider how and with whom you might share what you have received.

Bible in a year: Jeremiah 1,2; Psalms 112,113

A simple thing

PREPARE

Ask the Lord to speak to you as you read his Word today.

READ

2 Kings 5:1–27

EXPLORE

Naaman was proud, taking his request straight to the king, then being offended when Elisha didn't speak to him directly and getting angry when told to wash in the Jordan (vs 11,12). Yet he was also humble: twice allowing himself to be swayed by the advice of servants (vs 4,13), including a young, female foreigner (vs 2,3), whose opinions would have counted for nothing. I wonder how many times I have missed what God wants to say to me because I was too proud to listen to the person he chose to speak through.

We know well that we are saved by grace, yet how often do we still try to win God's favour with our gifts (v 5b) or by doing 'some great thing' (v 13), when all that is required is the simple act of trusting and obeying God? It is interesting that Elisha accepted a gift of food in yesterday's passage (4:42), but would not accept anything from

Naaman. The first was a free gift with no strings attached; Naaman's gift might have led him to believe that God's power could be purchased. This is why it mattered so much when Gehazi took something from Naaman (v 20): God's reputation was at stake. He and his servants were robbed of the full revelation that Israel's God is not swayed by wealth or status.

> '... if the prophet had told you to do some great thing, would you not have done it? How much more, then, when he tells you, "Wash and be cleansed"!'
>
> **2 Kings 5:13**

RESPOND

What are the simple things the Lord wants you to do?

Bible in a year: Jeremiah 3,4; John 2

[In]significant intervention

PREPARE

'Be still, and know that I am God' (Psalm 46:10).

READ

2 Kings 6:1–23

EXPLORE

The story about the axe-head is a strange one. It seems such a little thing. But for the man who had borrowed the axe (v 5), it was massive! God intervened and restored the axe-head so that the man could continue using it and return it to its owner.

In the next section (vs 8–23), God uses Elisha to foil the plans of an enemy army. Elisha received insight from God, then passed it to the king (v 9), and the king acted on this knowledge (v10). Elisha finds himself involved in world affairs, becoming the target of the enemy army (vs 12–14).

Sometimes I feel my prayers are mundane, small and even selfish. When I look at the big issues in the world – wars, famines, disease – it seems petty to ask the God of the universe for my little need. But when I think like that, I am imagining that God doesn't like to

be interrupted with something small because he's busy working on something big, or that somehow he can't multitask. It's as if I think God is like me when I'm preparing dinner and my children need help with a game or a craft: for them it's important, but for me it's a trivial interruption. God isn't human though: he can do both at once. Today's passage is a reminder that God is interested in our 'little' needs just as he is interested in major world events.

'... but Elisha, the prophet who is in Israel, tells the king of Israel the very words you speak in your bedroom.'

2 Kings 6:12

RESPOND

Pray one little prayer and one big prayer!

Bible in a year: Jeremiah 5,6; John 3

2 Kings 6:24 – 7:2

He is for you!

PREPARE

Thank God for the good things he has done this week.

· ·

READ

2 Kings 6:24 – 7:2

EXPLORE

What a dramatic change. In yesterday's passage the king of Israel trusted Elisha's words. In today's passage he appears to blame Elisha (v 31) for the siege and the suffering. To his credit, the king is distressed by the story he hears of women eating their children (v 30), but rather than take responsibility, he declares that God has caused the disaster (v 33b). The king considers that Elisha, as God's messenger, shares the blame (v 31).

When our disasters come, how do we react? Do we accuse the Lord of being the cause of our trouble? Or do we go to him for comfort, for guidance, for wisdom and in hope of a miracle? It depends on what we believe deep down about God. Although he'd previously seen God act for the good of Israel, the king believes that the Lord is against him. Elisha, on the other hand, has confidence that God will bring the siege

to a miraculous end (7:1,2). He knows that the Lord is *for* Israel.

Do you remember in the early months of the COVID-19 pandemic, when everything seemed scary and dark? Many churches, groups and nations recorded versions of a song called 'The Blessing' which carried a message we all desperately needed to hear: he is for you!

> Elisha replied, 'Hear the word of the LORD. This is what the LORD says ...'
>
> **2 Kings 7:1**

RESPOND

'In the morning, in the evening / In your coming, and your going / In your weeping, and rejoicing / He is for you, he is for you ...'*

*Jobe et al, © Worship Together Music, 2020

· ·

Bible in a year: Jeremiah 7,8; Psalms 114,115

Lost for words

PREPARE
If there is anything worrying you today, consciously lay it at the cross before you turn to the Scriptures.

....

READ
Psalm 113

EXPLORE
This psalm is divided into three parts. In the first (vs 1–3), we focus on the greatness, the vastness, the majesty, the impossible-to-describe-ness of God! We lift our eyes and catch a glimpse of just how amazing he is and find ourselves joining the psalmist in praise.

Lost for words, the psalmist seeks comparisons (vs 4–6), but finds that there are none. It's very hard to say 'God is like…' when actually he is in a completely different league from anything else in our experience.

In the final part of the psalm (vs 7–9), the psalmist gives examples of how this same incredible God deals with individuals. He doesn't show preference as the world would, but raises up those in need. Verse 9 really struck me, as I married and had children later than most. Reminiscing about that, I began to recall time after time when God has brought the miracles I needed: a job, an opportunity, a contact, even cash in the post! It is utterly mind-blowing to think that the Lord of all would care about my problem; that the King of kings knows each one of us so well that he can meet our personal precise need.

Who is like the LORD our God, the One who sits enthroned on high?
Psalm 113:5

RESPOND
Think of a time when the Lord answered your prayers and intervened in your life. Remember how it felt to know that the God of the universe cares for you. Thank him again.

....

Bible in a year: Jeremiah 9,10; John 4

Monday 9 October
2 Kings 7:3-20

Trusting his Word

Thank the Lord for the Bible.

. . . .

READ

2 Kings 7:3-20

EXPLORE

While there are plenty of lessons we can draw from this passage, verses 19 and 20 are clearly the moral the writer wants us to take from the story. The earlier exchange between Elisha and this servant (7:2) is retold and we are encouraged to reflect on the fulfilment of Elisha's words. I love how many times it is pointed out that this is what God had promised would happen (vs 16,17,18,19,20), to make sure that we get the message. It was an unpleasant conclusion for the officer concerned (v 17), but why is his death our lesson? The officer's sin was to doubt God, to suggest that God's word through Elisha could not be trusted.

The king, too, struggled to accept that God could have worked a miracle overnight, even though Elisha had told him it would happen (v 12). His suspicious mind caused him to create other possible reasons for the Arameans'

departure. Often, our tendency too is to be suspicious or doubtful when something good happens unexpectedly, especially when we have lost hope as the king had. Perhaps we don't see miracles often enough to expect them like Elisha did (v 1). Let's try to make a habit of thanking God when he intervenes on our behalf.

> It happened as the man of God had said to the king ...
>
> **2 Kings 7:18**

RESPOND

Which Bible promises are most significant for you right now? Maybe it's because you've seen them fulfilled, or perhaps because you are clinging on to them. Take time to meditate on them now, and thank the Lord that they are still true for you today.

. . . .

Bible in a year: Jeremiah 11,12; John 5

Constancy

PREPARE

Think of a Christian whose faith you admire. What are the qualities that stand out?

READ

2 Kings 8:1–29

EXPLORE

Yesterday we saw the consequences of not trusting in God's word. In the first part of today's passage (vs 1–6), we see God's faithfulness to the Shunammite woman when she acts according to his word. She does as Elisha says, is saved from the famine, and then receives blessing beyond what she had requested (v 6b).

The rest of the passage is a collection of kings with strange names, ruling over Israel, Judah and Aram. It's worth looking at a chart in your Bible or on the Internet to get your head around who's who, the time periods and how their reigns overlap. As in our day, there is a great deal of evil: so many things that would make us weep (vs 11,12). We see the kings of Judah and Israel doing evil in the sight of the Lord (vs 18,27), failing to teach the people to worship God.

As we reach the end of our series in 2 Kings, what strikes me is how Elisha has continued to minister over so many years. Thrones have changed their occupants, wars and famines have come and gone; Elisha has stayed faithful to his calling. His ministry has been the one constant in an ever-changing world. Well, not quite. Elisha has remained constant because he serves and trusts the unchanging God. God's longing for and jealousy towards his people has never faltered (v 19).

> 'Tell me about all the great things Elisha has done.'
>
> **2 Kings 8:4**

RESPOND

Reflect on God's faithfulness and unfailing love towards you.

Bible in a year: Jeremiah 13,14; John 6

Life's meaning and purpose

Ecclesiastes is a book of the Old Testament known as 'wisdom literature'. The identity of the author is not known, despite the detail in verse 1:1. The author created 'the teacher' to act as his voice. His main intention is to examine the meaning and purpose of life without God. He looks at wealth, pleasure, status and work as potential sources.

A recurring theme is that everything is meaningless or vanity (1:2 and 12:8), in the sense of being like a puff of smoke or wind that cannot be grasped, something that is temporary and fleeting. The phrase 'everything is meaningless under the sun' appears 38 times.

The teacher's answer is to accept that life is beyond our control. Wealth, pleasure, status and work are gifts from God and should be enjoyed to the full, even amid the fleeting nature of life.

The sense of God's presence becomes stronger in chapters 6 to 12. It is wisdom and fear of the Lord which provide meaning and purpose (see 7:13–18). Verses 11:7 to 12:7 see death as the great equaliser: wealthy, poor, wise or foolish people all die. The teacher's explorations and questions fall into place in chapter 12, verses 13 and 14 with the conclusion that humankind should fear God and keep his commandments.

Ecclesiastes may feel discouraging. However, it has a very contemporary ring because of the similarities with the world today, where so many people look to wealth, pleasure, status and career for meaning in their lives.

About the writer
Ali Walton

Ali is Associate Rector at Emmanuel Church, Loughborough. She is married to Steve. They share their home with a lovely Border Terrier called Flora. Ali enjoys reading, walking in the beautiful Leicestershire countryside and all things crafty and creative.

Chasing the wind

PREPARE
Where do you turn when life saps your energy, causing you to feel weary?

READ
Ecclesiastes 1:1–18

EXPLORE
Ecclesiastes 1 does not seem to say anything about God. Instead, everything is meaningless (v 2)! Some Bible versions use words such as vanity, futile, useless, nonsense or pointless. Read verse 2 again using each of those words. Think about how that helps you to understand the point. The original word used is more like a whisp of breath, a puff of smoke, an unseen breeze – something that is fleeting, short-lived, brief.

Three times 'the teacher' refers to 'life under the sun' (vs 3,9,14) to speak about life *without* God. He uses the phrase 'under the heavens' (v 12) for life *with* God. In the rest of this chapter he uses two examples for studying the meaning of life: creation (vs 3–11) and wisdom (vs 12–18). Look at these sections again. What might we learn?

Jesus summarises the meaning of Ecclesiastes 1 in Matthew 16:26. 'What good will it be for someone to gain the whole world, yet forfeit their soul? Or what can anyone give in exchange for their soul?' It does not matter how hard we work, or how much we know or have. If we live without God, we live in the futility of our own thinking (Ephesians 4:17).

> What has been will be again, what has been done will be done again; there is nothing new under the sun.
>
> Ecclesiastes 1:9

RESPOND
Culture encourages us to look for meaning in life in possessions, status and money. Where do you look for meaning in your life? Ask the Lord to give you strength to look to him alone.

Bible in a year: Jeremiah 15,16; Psalm 116

The meaning of life

PREPARE
What difference does it make to you that the Lord is with you? Thank him for his presence in your life.

READ
Ecclesiastes 2:1–26

EXPLORE
In chapter 2 the teacher turns to pleasure (vs 1–11), wisdom and folly (vs 12–16) and work (vs 17–23) as sources for meaning in life. Read each section carefully. Notice the things the teacher has tried doing to find meaning. He has taken some positives away from his experiment: he has delight in all his pleasures in life (v 10b); he realises that wisdom is better than folly (v 13); and he knows a person can do nothing better than work hard (v 24). It is not the case that these are wrong, but on their own they are not enough to provide meaning in life. In what ways do pleasure, wisdom and folly, and toil all fail to provide the meaning he is looking for?

Think about the context in which you live. Look for similarities between what the teacher says about the context in which he lived and yours. What do you notice?

The teacher does not end on a completely meaningless note. Verses 24 to 26 bring God into the picture. The teacher's conclusion (v 26) is that it is only in understanding that pleasure, wisdom and work are gifts from God that true meaning and happiness are to be found.

> To the person who pleases him, God gives wisdom, knowledge and happiness ...
>
> Ecclesiastes 2:26

RESPOND
How does this passage challenge you about where you look for meaning? You may want to say sorry to the Lord for times when you forget that he is the source of true meaning.

Bible in a year: Jeremiah 17,18; John 7

God, eternity and people

PREPARE
Read verse 11. How does it affect your view of life?

READ
Ecclesiastes 3:1–22

EXPLORE

Chapter 3 has three sections. Verses 1 to 8 explore 'seasons' of life. Verses 9 to 15 show that God is in control. Verses 16 to 22 remind us of our mortality.

The 'seasons' of life in verses 1 to 8 are pairs of opposites covering every aspect of life. How do these verses fit your life experience? The phrase 'under the heavens' is used to hint that God is in control. What difference does that make to you?

Verses 9 and 10 return to the theme of work being meaningless (see 2:17–23). However, verses 11 to 15 put our work in the context of our Creator God. Our work is temporary and meaningless when we try to control it to get the most profit out of it (vs 9,10). In contrast, work set in the context of God's eternity, seen as a gift from him (v 13), is satisfying.

The teacher explores judgement, justice and mortality in verses 16 to 22. The wicked and the righteous will be judged by God (v 17). Humans and animals are alike: both will die (v 19). The difference is that if humans see their lives and labour as gifts from God (v 13), they die having drawn satisfaction and joy from them. That, says the teacher, should be enough for us (vs 13,22).

> He has made everything beautiful in its time. He has also set eternity in the human heart; yet no one can fathom what God has done from beginning to end.
>
> **Ecclesiastes 3:11**

RESPOND
Think of someone you know who struggles with life. Pray for them to discover that with God their life has value and meaning.

Bible in a year: Jeremiah 19,20; John 8

Saturday 14 October
Ecclesiastes 4:1–16

Two are better than one

PREPARE

Think about the root cause of oppression. Pray for justice and mercy for oppressed people.

READ

Ecclesiastes 4:1–16

EXPLORE

This chapter confronts us with two ways to live: the way of greed, envy and abuse of power resulting in lonely wealth (vs 1–8), or the way of sharing, resulting in community and wisdom (vs 9–12).

Read verses 1 to 8 again carefully, looking for the causes and results of living for self and wealth. Envy and greed result in the poor, weak and needy being trampled on, abused and oppressed, in contradiction of Jewish Law (see Deuteronomy 24:14,15). The fool (v 5) who lives this way may be wealthy but ends up alone. This is summarised in verse 8. It's the result of people living in rebellion against God – 'the evil that is done under the sun' (vs 3,7).

Now read verses 9 to 12. Look for the reasons that prompt the teacher to say 'two are better than one' (v 9). It is striking that mutual cooperation and support result in a good return for work,

as well as companionship.

Verses 13 to 16 seem like a change of subject, yet, in contrasting the wealthy but lonely king with the poor but accompanied youth, the teacher illustrates what he has said about two ways to live. He concludes that poverty with wisdom is better than wealth without meaning.

> Two are better than one, because they have a good return for their labour.
>
> Ecclesiastes 4:9

RESPOND

Take an honest look at your own life. Confess the times when you live 'under the sun' and chase what you think benefits you. Ask the Lord for strength to live in a way that benefits others.

Bible in a year: Jeremiah 21,22; Psalms 117,118

Remember then, trust now

PREPARE

Remember when God has done something extraordinary for you. Thank him.

READ

Psalm 114

EXPLORE

Here is the core of Israel's identity as God's people. He rescued them from Egypt (v 1), formed them around his presence with them (v 2), and honed them through his rule over them (v 2).

Verses 3 and 4 are a reminder of the miraculous ways in which he controlled creation in order to save his people. He opened the Red Sea so they could escape safely (v 3; see Exodus 14:21,22), pushed back the River Jordan so they could cross safely into the Promised Land (v 3; see Joshua 3:14–16) and the mountains and hills trembled at God and his people coming to the land (v 4).

Verses 5 and 6 ask questions of the sea, river, mountains and hills which witnessed God's miraculous saving power. How would you answer?

Verses 7 and 8 consist of implicit challenges to faith. If the earth trembles at the presence of the Lord (v 7), then

so should God's people. If God were powerful enough to cause a lump of rock to become a life-saving spring of water (v 8; see Exodus 17:6), then surely he is powerful enough to save his people again. All the people need to do is continue to trust and hope in him.

Tremble, earth, at the presence of the Lord, at the presence of the God of Jacob.

Psalm 114:7

RESPOND

Bring to the Lord anything in your life that you're struggling to entrust to God. Remembering God's power, ask him to give you strength to trust and hope in him for this.

Bible in a year: Jeremiah 23,24; John 9

When is enough enough?

PREPARE

Spend a few moments asking the Lord to help you to listen to him today.

READ

Ecclesiastes 5:1–20

EXPLORE

In verses 1 to 7, the teacher addresses worshipping the Lord, rather than wealth and possessions. Worship involves treading on holy ground, and a desire to listen to the Lord. Fools (v 1) make offerings to the Lord, but with no real desire to engage with him. What other characteristics of worship do you see in these verses? Fearing God (v 7), in the sense of standing before him in silent awe and adoration, is key to worship.

Verses 8 to 17 return to the gathering of wealth at the expense of others as being meaningless. The teacher speaks about systemic, nationwide corruption in verses 8 and 9. Take a look at news headlines around you today. How might this passage prompt you to pray? Although written many years ago, these verses feel remarkably fresh and relevant for our world. Identify ways in which verses 8 to 17 speak into your context today.

Verses 18 to 20 provide the answer to the meaninglessness of verses 8 to 17. The teacher returns to the idea of work, pleasure and wealth being gifts from God. Verse 20 is particularly striking. Whereas those who seek wealth above all else end their days in darkness and frustration (v 17), those who see their work and wealth as gifts from God are too busy being contented and joyful to reflect on the meaning of life (v 20).

> Guard your steps when you go to the house of God. Go near to listen rather than to offer the sacrifice of fools ...
>
> Ecclesiastes 5:1

RESPOND

Pray for your government, that politicians may put the needs of others before their own wealth and glory.

Bible in a year: Jeremiah 25,26; John 10

What is wisdom?

PREPARE

Reflect on someone you consider wise. What prompts you to think this? Pray that you will learn wisdom as you read today's passage.

....

READ

Ecclesiastes 6:1 – 7:18

EXPLORE

The teacher again considers the point of prosperity (6:1–5). He puzzles over why some people cannot be content with what they have. He can't answer, and this inability leads him to ask more questions about the meaning of life (6:7–12). The only hint at an answer appears in verse 10, where he speaks of fighting with someone who is stronger – the implication being that this stronger person is God. Consider how you might answer such questions if asked them today.

Chapter 7, verses 1 to 14 consists of contrasts between wisdom and foolishness. Observe how the teacher describes the two. In verse 7 he notes how a person may become foolish, having been wise. What might these verses say about how to become wise? In verse 14 the teacher writes that God has made both good times and bad times. Think about how you would react to this statement in bad times.

Verse 15 points to another injustice in life. The teacher argues in verses 16 to 18 that a balance between wisdom and foolishness is essential. He concludes that fearing God (seeing the awesomeness of God) is the way to achieve it (v 18).

Wisdom, like an inheritance, is a good thing and benefits those who see the sun.

Ecclesiastes 7:11

RESPOND

Today's reading has covered a lot of ground. As you look back over it, think about one idea you want to take away. Ask the Lord to remind you of that for the rest of today.

....

Bible in a year: Jeremiah 27,28; John 11

Wisdom and faith

PREPARE
Today's reading is challenging. Ask the Lord to help you to understand it.

• •

READ
Ecclesiastes 7:19 – 8:17

EXPLORE
The teacher continues his writings about wisdom, reflecting on how it provides insight into human nature (7:19–22). But it is difficult to grasp. Wisdom cannot answer all our life-and-death questions (7:23,24). God's thoughts and control of the world are beyond us (see Isaiah 55:8,9). Yet, lack of wisdom leads to sinfulness (7:25–29). Using extremes common to his day, he concludes that wisdom is rare (7:28). Then, verse 29 forces us to look closely at our own hearts. How might these words apply in your life? The softening effect of wisdom (8:1) concludes this section.

Chapter 8 revisits the themes of Ecclesiastes 1:2 to 3:22. The teacher looks at the need to obey an unjust king (8:2–8) due to an oath of loyalty. Notice the other reasons given for tolerating an unjust ruler. Then he reflects on the injustices people suffer and the questions these raise (8:9–11,14). Yet, faith in God provides answers to the questions of meaning in life (8:12,13,15). We are reminded that joy can be found in work and pleasure when they are seen as God's gift (8:15). The teacher concludes that human wisdom is limited, and no one can fully understand the intricacies of life except God himself (8:16,17).

> Then I saw all that God has done. No one can comprehend what goes on under the sun. Despite all their efforts to search it out, no one can discover its meaning.
>
> **Ecclesiastes 8:17**

RESPOND
Read Isaiah 55:8,9 again. Ask the Lord to help you to trust him with the intricacies of your life.

• •

Bible in a year: Jeremiah 29–31; Psalm 119:1–24

Death, life, and wisdom

PREPARE

Think about where your hope in life comes from. Pray that God will strengthen your hope in him today.

....

READ

Ecclesiastes 9:1 – 10:11

EXPLORE

The teacher continues to explore big issues. One destiny awaits all people – good or evil – regardless of how people live (v 2). In these ancient times before Christ, the teacher seems not to have any expectation of life after death (9:3–6). Only the living have hope (v 4). Put yourself in the teacher's shoes and ponder what life without hope looks like.

Yet, despite 'this meaningless life ... under the sun' (9:9), the teacher believes it is possible to enjoy life. Look at 9:7. What difference does it make to see life in the context of God's unconditional love and acceptance?

Then the teacher contrasts wisdom and folly, describing how they differ (9:13–10:11). He provides an example of these at work in the story of the city under attack (9:13–18). He concludes that those who shout loudest may get noticed, even if they are foolish, whereas wise people are often ignored and forgotten. The different pictures in chapter 10, verses 1 to 11 might appear to be a series of disconnected proverbs, but read them again as contrasts between wisdom and foolishness. Try to identify what lesson for life the teacher is communicating through these. How might this influence your life now?

> Go, eat your food with gladness, and drink your wine with a joyful heart, for God has already approved what you do.
>
> Ecclesiastes 9:7

RESPOND

Thank the Lord for his unconditional love and acceptance. Pray that his love will help you to live life to the full (9:7) and fill you with hope.

....

Bible in a year: Jeremiah 32,33; John 12

Foolish or full?

PREPARE
Thank God that he holds the world in his hands, even when we are anxious.

• •

READ
Ecclesiastes 10:12 – 11:10

EXPLORE
In chapter 10, verses 12 to 20 the teacher returns to themes explored previously: what it is to be foolish (vs 12–15), and the effects of a foolish leader on national life (vs 16–20). List the characteristics and results of being foolish from verses 12 to 15. Notice the key to avoiding foolishness given in verse 12. Verses 16 to 19 look at the faults of a foolish leader and the implications for others. In verse 17 he hints at how wise leaders live. What are the differences between the two? Given the advice in verse 20, how might you pray for your leaders today?

Chapter 11 looks at how faith in God helps people to live full and joyful lives despite life's uncertainties – in those times, that particularly concerned agricultural issues (vs 1–6). Given the uncertainties you are facing, consider how verse 5 helps you to trust God today.

Light and seeing the sun (v 7) are used to refer to the joy of God's blessings

(see Psalm 97:11). Life and joy must be pursued actively because the dark days beyond death will soon come (v 8). God's judgement means that enjoyment of life should be in moderation (v 9). Yet, anxiety about life's big questions should not steal life and joy away, neither should age or lack of energy (v 10).

As you do not know the path of the wind, or how the body is formed in a mother's womb, so you cannot understand the work of God, the Maker of all things.

Ecclesiastes 11:5

RESPOND
Pray for wisdom for your local leaders. Pray that you will walk in the light of God's life and joy today.

• •

Bible in a year: Jeremiah 34,35; John 13

Remember your Creator

PREPARE
Recall doing something in your own strength, and something in God's strength. What was the difference?

READ
Ecclesiastes 12:1–14

EXPLORE
The teacher begins with instruction to young people to focus their lives on God, because ageing and death approach quickly: 'Remember your Creator in the days of your youth' (v 1). Verses 1 to 5 give a picture of ageing, describing the failure of our senses (vs 2–4), the loneliness of old age (v 4) and increasing physical frailty (v 5). Finally, verses 6 and 7 describe death. We are but dust, and to dust we shall return (v 7; see also Genesis 3:19). So the teacher repeats his opening reflection on life (v 8; see 1:2): 'Meaningless! Meaningless!'

In verses 9 to 14 the teacher and his teachings are recalled. Mention of the shepherd in verse 11 prompts thoughts about God as being more intimate than the Creator God of verse 1. Verse 12b is a well-known proverb. What do you think this might mean in the overall context of Ecclesiastes?

This leads to the teacher's conclusion (vs 13,14). His words provide an antidote to the meaninglessness and vanity of life without God, and of people living in their own strength (which the teacher has explored so thoroughly). Given all the big questions he has asked throughout the book, think about how satisfying his conclusion is for you.

Now all has been heard; here is the conclusion of the matter: fear God and keep his commandments, for this is the duty of all mankind.

Ecclesiastes 12:13

RESPOND
Ask the Lord to help you to live in his strength and not in your own, acknowledging that in this way lies fullness of life and joy.

Bible in a year: Jeremiah 36,37; Psalm 119:25–48

To God be the glory

PREPARE

Read Psalm 115:1. Praise the Lord for his love and faithfulness.

• •

READ

Psalm 115

EXPLORE

The idols of other nations are contrasted with the living God (vs 2–8). Our own world has many idols too! Using these verses, consider how you might answer someone who asks why they should worship the Lord and not idols of status, wealth or power. The words 'he is their help and shield' occur three times in verses 9 to 11: God provides help for his people and protects them. But idols cannot help because they have no power. These words challenge us today too with our tendency towards self-reliance. Only God can be our 'help and shield'.

Look at verses 12 to 15. Notice how often the words 'bless' or 'blessed' occur. The psalmist's words move from a sense of surviving (vs 9–11) to one of thriving. God gives abundantly to all his people. Verse 15 provides the reason for the declaration of praise in verse 1.

Praising the Lord continues (vs 16–18). Just as idols (see vs 4–8) are unable to praise God, neither can the dead (v 17). It is to the living that the Maker of heaven and earth gifts the earth; the living God gives help and provides protection and blessing to them. It is the living who praise the Lord now and always (v 18).

Not to us, LORD, not to us but to your name be glory, because of your love and faithfulness.

Psalm 115:1

RESPOND

What does the Lord's blessing look like in your life? Give him thanks for that. Pray for those you know who need the Lord's help today.

Bible in a year: Jeremiah 38,39; John 14

Scripture Union

FREE SUPPORTER PRAYER MAGAZINE

Connecting You with all God's doing through Scripture Union

Subscribe to *Connecting You* for FREE to get all the latest news and stories from Scripture Union + daily prayer pointers to help fuel your prayers.

SUBSCRIBE FOR FREE AT:
su.org.uk/connectingyou

Following blind

Following Jesus is simultaneously very straightforward and remarkably tricky. Just when you think you are beginning to get the hang of it, you stumble. Just when you feel you know him, your ignorance is exposed.

In these chapters we join the disciples in following Jesus. We do so with the advantage of knowing how the story ends. At times you may be shocked by their ignorance, inconsistency and frailty. If we're honest, we will recognise that they are no different from us.

It is widely thought that Mark was writing for the persecuted church in Rome and that he used the first-hand accounts of the apostle Peter to write his Gospel. Any failure of Christians there to follow Jesus well had huge implications for the whole community. In the same way, my discipleship will affect everyone with whom I am connected.

In the course of the journey, we are introduced to two blind men (chapters 8 and 10). Like them, the disciples struggle to see. They need to receive spiritual vision. It comes gradually and, until after the resurrection, incompletely. No wonder they stumble as Jesus leads them forward.

As readers, we can see how Mark is gradually revealing more and more about who Jesus is. This runs counter to the disciples' lack of perception. But following is different from understanding. It requires action. I hope that these notes will help you to follow Jesus with your eyes open.

About the writer
Steve Silvester

Steve is Rector of St Nic's Nottingham, a thriving, international, city-centre church. With his wife Jane, he is also a foster carer. In 2015, he founded Nottingham City Prayer, uniting churches across the city. Steve is a keen road cyclist and walker.

Heart of darkness

PREPARE
Read Ephesians 6:12. Where are you conscious of being in a spiritual battle? Are you aware of carrying some injuries? Or are you struggling to distinguish between 'flesh and blood' and 'spiritual forces'?

READ
Mark 5:1–20

EXPLORE
It had been a rough night. Jesus' disciples had thought they were going to drown until he calmed the storm. A man in a graveyard, overwhelmed by dark forces, was the last thing they needed.

The disciples were commissioned to drive out demons (3:15), but they are nowhere to be seen. Jesus is able to take the fight to the heart of darkness and win. Only Jesus has this kind of authority.

Our culture may have different ways to describe phenomena described here (mental illness, victim of abuse, etc). Naming is one thing; overcoming is quite another. Jesus brings peace to the man just as he had brought peace to the storm (v 15).

Another darkness hides behind this narrative. It's the darkness of a society that is more concerned about pigs and the economy than this man. He has been written off. The best they can do is try to contain him. When they see that Jesus is more powerful than the forces controlling this man whom they could not tame, the townsfolk are terrified. Their request to Jesus to leave the region shows what side of this titanic struggle they are really on.

> When they came to Jesus, they saw the man who had been possessed by the legion of demons, sitting there, dressed and in his right mind.
> **Mark 5:15**

RESPOND
Pray for the gift of discernment. It is not easy to accurately identify evil. Do we scapegoat people? Do we sometimes focus on individuals and miss structural evil?

Bible in a year: Jeremiah 40,41; John 15

Mark 5:21–34

No hiding

PREPARE

When an old farmer was asked what he did when he went into the church to pray, he replied, 'Nothing, I look at him, and he looks at me.' Are you ready to meet with God like this?

READ

Mark 5:21–34

EXPLORE

This woman faces a dilemma: she believes that she can be healed if she can just touch Jesus (see also 3:10; 6:56), but scripture forbade contact with anyone in her state (Leviticus 15:25–33). So physical contact with Jesus is both the one thing she desperately needs and the one thing she must not do. This explains the sly way she went about things.

The fact that she was healed, and instantly knew that she was, may have added to her alarm when Jesus called her to identify herself, because it testified to the awesome power of Jesus.

Jesus insists on knowing who has intentionally touched his clothing. The woman's response is to come forward and tell him the whole truth. In this way, Jesus rehabilitates this woman into society: no longer unclean, she can be close to people again. More importantly, Jesus'

actions make this a personal encounter. He insists that the woman is seen and known. Jesus is not content to be a holy battery discharging power anonymously.

> Then the woman, knowing what had happened to her, came and fell at his feet and, trembling with fear, told him the whole truth.
>
> Mark 5:33

RESPOND

You cannot come to Jesus hiding behind low self-esteem, shame or a sense of unworthiness. Nor can you use him as a means to an end, a distant distributor of answers to your problems. Look Jesus in the eye and make the encounter personal.

Bible in a year: Jeremiah 42,43; John 16

God's doorkeeper

PREPARE

Dietrich Bonhoeffer famously wrote, 'Only believers obey; only the obedient believe.' Our beliefs are not measured by our statements, but by our actions. Review the past week in the light of this thought.

READ

Mark 5:35–43

EXPLORE

Jesus told the woman he met on the way to Jairus' house, '… your faith has healed you …' (v 34). Now he tells Jairus, '… just believe' (v 36).

Faith plays a key role in Jesus' healing miracles. Jesus was restricted by the lack of faith of his home town (Mark 6:6); elsewhere faith seemed to unlock healing. If someone is healed, we cannot take credit because we believed; nor can we say, 'You were not healed because you didn't have enough faith.' But if faith is in the mix, whether it is the faith of the person who is sick or of the person who loves them, the atmosphere changes.

One commentator uses this striking phrase: 'Faith opens the door to the power of God.'* It is not that faith is the power that heals, but it lets the power of God in.

As they make the long walk to Jairus' home, Jesus encourages him to play his part. As a father he would do anything for his 'little daughter' (v 23). The best, and only, thing he could do for her was to put his faith in Jesus.

> Overhearing what they said, Jesus told him, 'Don't be afraid; just believe.'
>
> Mark 5:36

RESPOND

Who is on your heart at this time? Rather than focusing on the problem they face, hold them before Jesus and pay attention to his kindness and power.

*DE Garland, *The NIV Application Commentary (Mark)*, Zondervan, 1996, p227

Bible in a year: Jeremiah 44–46; Psalm 119:49–72

Hidden in plain sight

PREPARE

Pray: 'Lord, open my eyes to your glory. Deliver me from distraction and overfamiliarity. Clean the lens of my spiritual vision.'

READ

Mark 6:1–13

EXPLORE

It isn't often that you read of Jesus being surprised, but the lack of faith he found in his home town shocked him. Overfamiliarity made the Son of God invisible. People saw the local carpenter; the brother to a large group of siblings; the son of Mary, whose husband seems to have died. 'We all know Jesus.' So today, many people have 'moved on' from Jesus to try more exotic spiritualities.

Jesus always resisted self-advertisement. Because of the reality of the incarnation, of God truly becoming fully human in Jesus, anyone could look at him and see 'just another bloke'. But these stories show that the problem lies with the observer. When people lack faith to approach Jesus for help, his true identity remains hidden from them.

By contrast, Christians are often tempted to impress and, in so doing,

they actually conceal the work of God. Jesus sends the disciples without bread, money, spare clothes or begging bowls. Their evident lack of resources, and being so unimpressive, would make the power of God more evident when they preached, cast out demons and anointed people for healing.

> He was amazed at their lack of faith.
>
> Mark 6:6

RESPOND

You may know people who grew up in the church but who no longer show any interest in Jesus. Or there may be people who just roll their eyes when Jesus is mentioned. Pray for revelation, that they would see him for who he is.

Bible in a year: Jeremiah 47,48; John 17

Pulling strings

PREPARE
Do you sometimes feel like a puppet – that other people are controlling you, 'pulling your strings'? Bring those situations to God now.

READ
Mark 6:14–29

EXPLORE
Here, Mark uses one of his favourite literary techniques, 'bracketing' – sandwiching a seemingly unrelated incident between two sections of his narrative. Why interject this flashback to the grisly murder of John the Baptist? It casts a shadow over the success of the disciples' mission, which is what Mark intends.

So many events in life – some with profound and lasting impact – derive not from well thought-out plans, but from the capricious actions of very flawed people. A boss's bad mood, or a political leader's opportunism, can have devastating effects. Even Jesus was affected by such things. Like John, Jesus will be executed by a man who makes a promise that backfires (15:9). Like John, he will be 'handed over' (10:33) when a devious figure behind the scenes finds an 'opportune time' (14:11). Moreover, in chapter 13, Jesus will warn his disciples that they should expect similar treatment.

So we live in this tension: the kingdom of God flashes in as people respond to the good news and are healed (vs 12,13,30), but the shadow of the cross is a constant reality. It is produced by the actions of ordinary people whose ambitions and lusts make them puppets in the hands of darker forces.

Finally the opportune time came.

Mark 6:21

RESPOND
John the Baptist was not raised from the dead (v 14), but Jesus was! Though we may not see it now, God's purposes transcend human whims. Be encouraged. Ultimately, his will prevails (see Genesis 50:20).

Bible in a year: Jeremiah 49,50; John 18

In whose hands?

PREPARE

Read 2 Corinthians 12:9. What is God saying to you through this?

READ

Mark 6:30–44

EXPLORE

The Jewish reader of this passage would be reminded of someone else who was responsible for a huge group of people in a desert, who taught them the things of God and who provided 'bread' (manna) for them. Knowing he could lead people only so far, Moses prayed that God would provide someone who would be able to lead them into the full blessings he had in store for them, '... so that the Lord's people will not be like sheep without a shepherd' (Numbers 27:15–17). It was not Joshua, son of Nun, who would lead people into the fullness of God's blessing, but Jesus, Son of God.

This incident marks another steep learning curve for Jesus' disciples. They have learned to minister to people spiritually (and to have their own physical needs provided for by their hosts). But Jesus meets people's spiritual *and* physical needs. Now he tells them, 'You give them something to eat.'

Confronted with this impossible command, they learn a profound secret of the kingdom of God: if we give our limited resources to Jesus, they will be multiplied. Like an old instrument in the hands of a gifted musician, or meagre ingredients in the hands of a master chef, what matters is not the scale of our resources, but whose hands they are in.

Taking the five loaves and the two fish ... he gave thanks and broke the loaves ... They all ate and were satisfied.

Mark 6:41,42

RESPOND

Pray: 'Lord Jesus, I place into your hands my ordinariness, my limitations, my few resources. Use them today to feed any hungry and lost people I meet.'

Bible in a year: Jeremiah 51,52; Psalm 119:73–96

Make the ask!

PREPARE

Take time to let the deep prayer of your heart surface. Write it down on a piece of paper. Carry this round with you and pray it through the day.

READ

Psalms 116,117

EXPLORE

Psalm 116 is a powerful song of personal testimony; Psalm 117 addresses the whole of humanity. Connecting the two is the character of God who is faithful and loving. We know this through personal experience, but it is a 'public truth' not just a private value.

If Psalm 117 tells the nations to acknowledge God, Psalm 116 tells individuals to call on him through the challenges of personal experience. The psalmist seems to have called on God in a moment of desperation (vs 3,4), and God has answered him. His response is to call on God more and more (v 2). He becomes a 'call on the Lord' enthusiast (vs 13,17), his faith moving in an upward spiral.

I wonder whether we are sometimes too polite in our relationship with God. Jesus never turned away anyone who came to ask him for things. In fact, he urged some people to articulate a request that was obvious (see Mark 10:51). James tells his readers, 'You do not have because you do not ask God' (James 4:2,3), but also warns that we need to ask with the right motives.

> Return to your rest, my soul, for the LORD has been good to you.
>
> **Psalm 116:7**

RESPOND

'What do you want me to do for you?' How would you reply if Jesus asked you this question? Is it time for you to call on the Lord so you can find rest for your soul (v 7)?

Bible in a year: Lamentations 1,2; John 19

Going nowhere

PREPARE

Are you rowing into a headwind, or is the wind in your sails right now? Reflect on these words: 'When you pass through the waters, I will be with you' (Isaiah 43:2).

READ

Mark 6:45–56

EXPLORE

Jesus needed time alone with his Father (v 46; see also 1:35). So do we. Up on the hillside, he can see his disciples straining on the oars. This is a wonderful picture of Jesus now. Risen and exalted, he sees when I am struggling. He is still interceding for us (Romans 8:34).

Jesus makes his disciples go ahead without him. They aren't in danger, but they are going nowhere. Sometimes we hit times when life is just hard going. Where is Jesus? Why doesn't he deal with the headwinds that make life such a struggle? Despite the disciples' situation, he intends to 'pass by them' (v 48). To us, this is puzzling. However, a wider look at the Bible shows that Jesus has a bigger agenda than solving his disciples' problems.

In wanting to 'pass by', Jesus is wanting to show them his glory. God 'passed by' Moses (Exodus 33:19 – 34:7) and Elijah

(1 Kings 19:11,12). Jesus does what only God can do (Job 9:8). But the disciples are characteristically blind to the revelation in front of them, just as they had been when Jesus had fed the 5,000 (v 52). Their progress is slow.

> He saw the disciples straining at the oars, because the wind was against them. Shortly before dawn he went out to them, walking on the lake. He was about to pass by them ...
>
> Mark 6:48

RESPOND

The Lord wants to reveal his glory to his people. For Moses, Elijah and the disciples he did this when life was challenging. Remember the Lord may have a bigger intention than making life easier for you.

Bible in a year: Lamentations 3–5; John 20

Cleanliness and godliness

PREPARE

Take some time to pray this prayer: 'Create in me a pure heart, O God, and renew a steadfast spirit within me' (Psalm 51:10).

READ

Mark 7:1–23

EXPLORE

Most parents teach their children to wash their hands before eating. This is because science tells us that certain bacteria we come into contact with can be dangerous if consumed. For the Pharisees, the washing of hands before meals was for a different reason. They wanted to live as people set apart for God, to be 'clean' in a ceremonial, not hygienic, way. They even adopted some rituals prescribed for priests in the Temple (see Exodus 30:19–21).

As their world was increasingly threatened by an alien (Hellenistic) culture, it was important to live out their distinctiveness in everyday life. So why would Jesus allow his disciples to adopt lower standards?

Jesus makes it clear that 'cleanliness' is a matter of the heart (v 21). The actions he cites (vs 21,22) can be avoided, but the attitudes he lists easily contaminate. It's relatively easy to keep yourself clean of adultery and murder, but greed, malice, deceit and arrogance tend to get under the fingernails.

So what does it mean for us to be 'distinctive' as Christians today? Do we focus on the right things? Are we different from society in ways that are attractive and point to God, or are we open to the accusation of being prudish, petty and irrelevant?

He went on: 'What comes out of a person is what defiles them. For it is from within, out of a person's heart, that evil thoughts come …'
Mark 7:20,21

RESPOND

Have you noticed anything 'coming out of you' (words, reactions) that suggest that there are things inside that need cleaning?

Bible in a year: Ezekiel 1; John 21

Unstoppable

PREPARE
Read 1 Kings 8:27 and use this as a basis for praise and worship as you come into his presence.

READ
Mark 7:24–37

EXPLORE

These two stories are about Jesus' ministry crossing boundaries. Mark underlines the woman's Gentile identity (v 26). Galileans resented Tyre. It was a wealthy city that ate their much-needed grain. If Jesus was Israel's expected Messiah, why waste time there?

The surprise in the first story is not how Jesus speaks to the woman, but how she responds (v 28). She shows more understanding than the disciples (Mark 6:52) and more humility than Jesus' Jewish listeners. She is prepared to be the 'little dog' snatching crumbs of food falling from 'the children's table'. Jesus recognises her determination to cross religious boundaries out of concern for her daughter, and he responds with generous kindness.

The deaf-mute man is also from a Gentile area (vs 31,32). Jesus saw his mission as being 'first to the Jews', as did Paul (Romans 1:16; 2:9). He went to Tyre to be alone, not to perform miracles. But the good news, once announced, starts an unstoppable process of reaching wider and wider.

As Peter found when he invited Jesus to his home (Mark 1:29–34), where Jesus is present, people will come 'so that the grace that is reaching more and more people may cause thanksgiving to overflow to the glory of God' (2 Corinthians 4:15).

> … yet he could not keep his presence secret.
>
> Mark 7:24

RESPOND

Do we sometimes try to contain the good news about Jesus? Are we afraid of what may happen if 'the wrong sort of people' gain access to him?

Bible in a year: Ezekiel 2,3; Psalm 119:97–120

Blinded by preconceptions

PREPARE

Pray: 'Let me seek you in my desiring, let me desire you in my seeking. Let me find you by loving you, let me love you when I find you' (St Anselm).

READ

Mark 8:1–13

EXPLORE

Were you tempted to skip over this section? It looks remarkably similar to the feeding of the 5,000 in chapter 6. Is it necessary? Has Mark included it by mistake? Be careful! Your preconceptions can make you miss the obvious.

Having seen Jesus feed the 5,000, how could the disciples imagine that he would not feed this crowd? Although the two feeding miracles are similar in many ways, there is one crucial difference. The first took place in a Jewish area, whereas this incident takes place in a Gentile area. The disciples expected Jesus to provide for Israel, but they didn't seem to expect him to be Messiah for everyone else.

Jesus' implicit claim to be the Saviour of the world may have been behind the Pharisees' demand for a sign from heaven (v 11). Sceptical of Jesus' claims unless substantiated by God, they believed that the true Messiah would smash Israel's enemies. But Jesus keeps moving on (vs 10,13) and will not be boxed in. The only way to understand Jesus is to keep moving with him, constantly open to new discoveries.

'I have compassion for these people; they have already been with me three days and have nothing to eat.'

Mark 8:2

RESPOND

Do you have preconceptions that blind you to the heart of Jesus? Pray: 'Lord, wash the window of my mind, so that I can see clearly again. Help me to be attentive to you and to catch the nuances of your voice. Amen.'

Bible in a year: Ezekiel 4,5; James 1

Join the dots

PREPARE

Take some time to review the past week or month. What might God be wanting to teach you? Can you see any patterns emerging?

· ·

READ

Mark 8:14–21

EXPLORE

In their frequent crossings of the lake, a boat serves as a classroom for Jesus' disciples. However, they seem to keep missing the point he wants to teach them. In chapter 4 (vs 35–41), they are so terrified of the storm that they fail to grasp Jesus' power until he has calmed the water. They lack faith. In chapter 6 (vs 45–52), they are filled with fear as Jesus walks to them on the water because 'they had not understood about the loaves; their hearts were hardened' (6:52). Now Jesus takes them back to the two miraculous feedings and they still don't get it. Their hearts are hardened; they don't remember (v 18).

Jesus wants to warn them against the insidious unbelief of the Pharisees and the followers of Herod. These are people who see what Jesus *does*, but fail to join the dots to see who he *is*. The disciples are running the same risk. They fail to see the maths of the kingdom: the less Jesus has to work with, the more he produces! He himself is the bread we all need (see John 6:35).

> 'Do you have eyes but fail to see, and ears but fail to hear? And don't you remember?'
>
> Mark 8:18

RESPOND

Might your commute to work, or regular trip to the shops, be the classroom in which Jesus is trying to teach you? Pray for the ability to see his hand at work, and your heart to be open to revelations of who he is.

· ·

Bible in a year: Ezekiel 6,7; James 2

Believing is seeing

PREPARE
Pray: 'Lord, I pray that the eyes of my heart may be enlightened in order that I may know the hope to which you have called me. Amen' (see Ephesians 1:18).

READ
Mark 8:22–30

EXPLORE
The two-stage healing of this blind man may surprise us. Jesus seems to be wrestling with the blindness. After the initial act of healing, like a modern doctor, Jesus asks his patient whether he can see anything before giving him additional 'treatment'. Jesus is not satisfied with his patient being able to see vague moving shapes (v 24).

This incident helps us interpret the next event, Peter's 'revelation' of the true identity of Jesus (v 29). Looking ahead to verse 33, we can see that Peter does not yet have 20:20 vision. He will not see clearly (v 25) until after Jesus' death and resurrection. He sees that Jesus is the Messiah, but that's through the blurred lens of his preconceptions. For Jesus, bringing true spiritual sight to his disciples is a prolonged struggle.

Sometimes we talk with friends and family as if coming to faith depended entirely on them (or on what we say to them). People can arrive at the first stage of spiritual perception through reason, evidence or experience. But a true understanding of Jesus requires revelation because it engages our whole person, not just our mind.

> He looked up and said, 'I see people; they look like trees walking around.'
>
> Mark 8:24

RESPOND
Even Christians can fool themselves into thinking that they 'get' Jesus, but there is so much more to discover. Read 1 Corinthians chapter 13, verse 12. How do you now want to pray for yourself and others?

Bible in a year: Ezekiel 8,9; Psalm 119:121–144

Staying on track

PREPARE
Galatians 5:25 urges us to 'keep in step with the Spirit'. Are you in danger of lagging behind or rushing ahead? Take time to get in step.

READ
Psalm 119:1–24

EXPLORE
Last year my wife and I walked the coast-to-coast path across England. Our main concern was about my navigation and its potential impact on our relationship! We were saved by downloading the route for each day on my phone. So long as the red triangle (indicating our GPS position) was on the red line of the route, all was well. If we were ever in doubt, we could zoom in to get a more detailed map.

For the psalmist, the 'law of the LORD' is his map. He wants his 'way' to be perfect (v 1) and steadfast (v 5), staying on the path of purity (v 9). He wants to access as much detail as possible (v 18) so that he can walk with confidence and integrity. He is determined to memorise the route, so he won't go off track (v 11).

At times we are unsure of which way to go. Is the map of the Word of God really reliable? We may be tempted to use our own judgement or to listen to directions from other authoritative voices (v 23), but the safest way is to let the map guide you (v 24).

> Blessed are those whose ways are blameless, who walk according to the law of the LORD.
>
> Psalm 119:1

RESPOND
In the Bible the image of 'walking' is more about a way of life than about geography or biography. Spend some time praying about what you are becoming, as well as what you are doing.

Bible in a year: Ezekiel 10,11; James 3

Public shame, public glory

PREPARE

Read Isaiah 53:1-6 and turn it into thanks to Jesus.

READ

Mark 8:31 – 9:1

EXPLORE

Peter says to Jesus, 'Lord, I'd like a word with you in private' (see v 32). Having earlier affirmed that Jesus is the Messiah (v 29), Peter feels the need to spell out to him what this means. In Peter's mind, this was not a title associated with suffering and death.

Jesus suddenly turns this private moment into a very public correction of Peter, not only before the full group of disciples but also the crowd (v 34). Suffering is an integral part of Jesus' own destiny, and it is also an essential part of being his disciple. This is not a secret, private matter. Followers of Jesus will need to publicly acknowledge their allegiance to a suffering Messiah, and this will entail risking the same rejection and abuse (vs 34,35).

People need to know this before they take even the first step in following him. The paradox at the heart of following Jesus is this: true life, the life of the kingdom, is possible only when the old life dies (vs 35-37). This has to be worked out in full view of our contemporaries, just as the eventual rule of the Messiah will be public and visible (v 38). In fact, it will be visible even in Jesus' crucifixion and resurrection (9:1).

… 'Whoever wants to be my disciple must deny themselves and take up their cross and follow me.'

Mark 8:34

RESPOND

Have you turned your allegiance to Jesus into a private, internal matter? How is he calling you to acknowledge him in front of your contemporaries? How can verse 38 help you face the possible consequences?

Bible in a year: Ezekiel 12,13; James 4

A break in the clouds

PREPARE

Can you make Psalm 27:8 your prayer today? 'My heart says of you, "Seek his face!" Your face, LORD, I will seek.'

READ

Mark 9:2–13

EXPLORE

You may have climbed a mountain in low cloud, then, as the mist clears, enjoyed a wonderful panorama. Things that had always been real suddenly became visible. In this passage, Jesus' closest disciples (see 5:37–43; 14:33) are invited to accompany him up a mountain, but it is when the cloud descends that they have a chance to see clearly.

Moses, Israel's first liberator, and Elijah, whom Jews expected before the final coming of the kingdom of God (see v 11), join Jesus on the mountain. There are many echoes of Moses' experience in Exodus 24 here, but Jesus is greater than Moses.

Unlike Moses, Jesus will liberate people through his death and resurrection (vs 9–13). Jesus is constantly trying to tell his disciples this (8:31,32; 9:30–32), but the cloud of ignorance still lingers. Even this experience leaves them confused. Fundamentally, they need to learn to be quiet and listen to Jesus (v 7). As he tries to point them towards his death (vs 9–13), they struggle to connect this with his glory. John, in his Gospel, makes it clear that only if Jesus is 'lifted up' on a cross will he be 'lifted up' in glory (John 12:32).

> 'This is my Son, whom I love. Listen to him!'
>
> Mark 9:7

RESPOND

If our heart is not inclined to listen to Jesus, even the most impactful experience of his presence can leave us confused and ignorant. Is there something he's trying to say that we avoid hearing?

Bible in a year: Ezekiel 14,15; James 5

Learning the hard way

PREPARE
Our failures are painful, but they can be the most fruitful sources of learning. As you ponder this statement, which experiences spring to mind?

READ
Mark 9:14–29

EXPLORE
Jesus had trained his disciples to cast out demons. Already they had had some success (6:7,13), but here is a noisy scene of controversy and failure (vs 14–18). At the heart of it is a desperate father and his sick son. Whatever contemporary medical label we might give to the boy's condition, the underlying cause is evil. What is going on, and why are the disciples so ineffective?

Like us today, Jesus was operating in a climate of unbelief (v 19). The struggle in this scene is not with the powers of evil, but with unbelief. The disciples do not need to hone their technique: they need stronger faith. Jesus is able to work even with the mixture of faith and unbelief which the boy's father confesses (v 24).

The key lesson for the disciples is that something else underpins faith: prayer (v 29). While desparate, even loud, energetic prayer in the face of evil has a place, Jesus ' secret is the ongoing background current of prayer that expresses total dependence on God, the essence of faith (1:35). With this, when evil rears its head, he is ready and equipped.

> He replied, 'This kind can come out only by prayer.'
>
> Mark 9:29

RESPOND
The causes of public failure rarely lie in the immediate circumstances. Track back from the failures you have recalled. What is the Lord trying to teach you?

Bible in a year: Ezekiel 16,17; Psalm 119:145–176

Ego havoc

PREPARE
Who do you know who most embodies humility? Thank God for them.

READ
Mark 9:30-50

EXPLORE

If you were to see Jesus walking through Galilee ahead of his disciples, you would notice a stark contrast. Jesus knows that he is heading towards suffering, death and resurrection (v 31). In obedience to his father, he will give his life as a ransom for many (10:45). His priority is to help his disciples understand this, and the implications for following him. Instead, as he walks alone, his disciples quarrel about where they fit in the pecking order (v 34). Such is their self-regard that they object to others casting out demons in Jesus' name (v 38), even though they have just failed to exorcise a young boy.

Egotism destroys community and makes us dangerous to others, especially the weak and the vulnerable (see v 42). Jesus tells his disciples to deal savagely with these tendencies (vs 43–48). Within the community of Jesus, true greatness is radically redefined as being like a child who, in Jesus' day, had no status, no power and few rights. Jesus, on his lonely walk to the cross, embodies this greatness. His attitude is the pattern for all who would follow him (see Philippians 2:1–11).

Humility is the 'salt' that keeps the community healthy, which perfects the sacrifice of lives given to God (see Leviticus 2:13), and which enables fellowship. Once it has gone, it is hard to restore.

'Anyone who wants to be first must be the very last, and the servant of all.'

Mark 9:35

RESPOND
Reflect on these words:
'Humble yourselves, therefore, under God's mighty hand, that he may lift you up in due time' (1 Peter 5:6).

Bible in a year: Ezekiel 18,19; 1 Peter 1

Hard-hearted

PREPARE

Pray: 'Come, Holy Spirit, and soften my heart. I am here before you, ready to listen.'

. . . .

READ

Mark 10:1–12

EXPLORE

The Pharisees' question is odd. The Old Testament teaching was clear (see Deuteronomy 24:1–4). A man was permitted to divorce his wife, but, if she remarried and was divorced again, he could not marry her for a second time. This was to protect the woman from wife-swapping. Both could marry another person without the accusation of adultery.

These can be hard verses to read if you have been through a divorce. It is important to note that Jesus is speaking with men who saw women as disposable. He is avoiding being dragged into a debate over particular reasons for divorce. He is not issuing pastoral guidance. Human experience testifies to the truth he is emphasising: God's will is for marriage to be permanent, and when a marriage breaks down a clean separation is almost impossible. Part of one's 'flesh' tends to remain stuck to the former spouse.

Maybe the Pharisees were trying to lure Jesus into making a controversial statement that could land him in trouble with Herod, like John the Baptist (6:14). Their approach to divorce centred on the question, 'What can I get away with?' For Jesus, the issue is not legislation on marriage, but the attitude of the heart (v 5), and this applies whether you are married, divorced or single.

'It was because your hearts were hard that Moses wrote you this law,' Jesus replied.

Mark 10:5

RESPOND

Pray for marriages you know, and for adults and children affected by divorce.

. . . .

Bible in a year: Ezekiel 20,21; 1 Peter 2

Open-handed

PREPARE

Take a look at your hands. What do they say about your life experience? What might the hands of Jesus, used in blessing children, have looked like?

READ

Mark 10:13–16

EXPLORE

It is interesting that this incident, involving children, follows immediately after the dispute about divorce. In adult conflicts, children are often the innocent victims. Not that Jesus would have our romantic view of childhood. Children can be just as spiteful, selfish and annoying as adults. The point here is that they are powerless. In Jesus' day, children had no status at all.

These children are almost the mirror-image of the rich man who approaches Jesus next (see Monday's note). They have to be brought to Jesus. They have no achievements to boast of; they are not looking for anything to 'do'. They simply receive Jesus' touch and blessing. Maybe this is why Jesus makes children the model for the kingdom of God. It is their capacity to receive that he emphasises.

Jesus himself was comfortable receiving. He received hospitality from a tax collector (2:15), extravagant affection from a woman (14:3) and even someone else's tomb (15:46). Sometimes we equate maturity with independence and self-sufficiency. This does not seem to be Jesus' view (v 15).

'Truly I tell you, anyone who will not receive the kingdom of God like a little child will never enter it.'

Mark 10:15

RESPOND

How do you feel about receiving from others – and from God? Are you selective in your thinking about who has something to offer you? We can be open-handed in our giving – but may be less so in receiving. Spend some time in prayer, hands open, before God now.

Bible in a year: Ezekiel 22,23; Psalms 120–122

The long trail

PREPARE
Read 2 Timothy 4:7. Thank God for people you know who have 'run well'.

READ
Psalm 119:25–48

EXPLORE
This remarkable psalm seems to say the same thing again and again. The psalmist wants his life to be shaped by the will of God: to run 'in the way of your commands' (vs 32,35). But this is a long trail. We hear the same rhythmic prayer, like footsteps, but the terrain constantly changes.

In these sections, the psalmist is 'laid low in the dust' (v 25). He is 'weary with sorrow' (v 28). He senses that he could be in mortal, or spiritual, danger and cries out, '… preserve my life …' (vs 25,37).

The challenges of the spiritual life are not constant. They change with circumstances and age. Here, the psalmist is conscious of his susceptibility to deceit and temptation (vs 29,36,37).

Athletes break down their races into stages, even a 100-metre sprint that lasts only 10 seconds. Maybe we need to pay more attention to the stage of the

'race' or 'walk' of our spiritual life. Yes, we want to keep putting one foot in front of the other, seeking to be shaped by his will. But what is this particular season about? What does faithfulness look like in this stage of my life?

> Direct me in the path of your commands, for there I find delight.
>
> Psalm 119:35

RESPOND
'As we progress in this way of life and in faith, we shall run on the path of God's commandments, our hearts overflowing with the inexpressible delight of love' (Prologue, Rule of St Benedict). Make these words a prayer for this stage of your life.

Bible in a year: Ezekiel 24,25; 1 Peter 3

Obvious candidate

PREPARE

Reflect on these words: 'Only Jesus Christ, who bids us follow him, knows where the path will lead. But we know that it will be a path full of mercy beyond measure. Discipleship is joy' (Dietrich Bonhoeffer).

READ

Mark 10:17–31

EXPLORE

Why would Jesus not welcome this potential recruit with open arms? He is eager, virtuous and rich enough to fund Jesus' fragile movement. Wouldn't you want him in your church? But Jesus sees through him. He is keen to be 'good', and so obtain eternal life. But only God is good. The very thought that he can 'do' anything to obtain eternal life is a joke.

Jesus' response to this man could seem harsh were it not for one short sentence: 'Jesus looked at him and loved him' (v 21). Is it really loving to demand so much of him? When my daughter was going travelling, she asked me to check her rucksack. As I set aside item after item, she cried, 'Dad, I can't do without *that*!' On her return, she said she wished I'd been even more ruthless! 'I had so many things I didn't need. They just weighed me down.'

The disciples may not have been as virtuous as this man, but they had 'left everything' to follow Jesus. They left their families but gained a new family; they left fields, but had become more fruitful (with persecution thrown in). Jesus still looks for more than respect and zealous attempts to lead a good life. He's all or nothing.

> Then Peter spoke up, 'We have left everything to follow you!'
>
> Mark 10:28

RESPOND

What is Jesus saying to you about following him? How serious are you?

Bible in a year: Ezekiel 26,27; 1 Peter 4

Leading the way

PREPARE
Think of a time when you had to follow someone, by car or on foot. What emotions did you experience at the different stages of the journey? How do you feel about following Jesus right now?

. . . .

READ
Mark 10:32–45

EXPLORE
Maybe it was because Jesus chose them first (Mark 1:16–20) that James and John expected preferential rewards for following Jesus. They may have had Psalm 110 verse 1 in mind as they anticipated Jesus' glory.

Jesus is leading the way (v 32) directly to the cross. After his resurrection he will continue to lead the way (Mark 14:28; 16:7). This trajectory – to suffering before glory – will continue to be the heart of what it means to follow him. He made this clear (eg 8:34,35), but his disciples seem incapable of absorbing this reality. They are astonished as he heads to Jerusalem.

Power is seductive. Regimes change all the time, but unless there is a radical shift in attitudes to power, one oppressive government will simply be changed for another. At the heart of

Jesus' kingdom is the reverse of what people normally associate with 'leading' (vs 42–44). Jesus' leadership serves rather than dominates, and liberates rather than enslaves (v 45).

'For even the Son of Man did not come to be served, but to serve, and to give his life as a ransom for many.'

Mark 10:45

RESPOND
Pray: 'I have decided to follow you, Lord Jesus, but I'm so often the straggler, the wanderer, the one who disputes your navigation, even challenges your right to lead. Here, now, I fall into line. Lead on, Lord.'

. . . .

Bible in a year: Ezekiel 28,29; 1 Peter 5

Model disciple

PREPARE

Can you think of someone who has just started the Christian journey? What can you learn from them? Do they have something that you have lost?

READ

Mark 10:46–52

EXPLORE

For nearly a month we have been following the progress of Jesus' disciples. They have been so slow to appreciate who Jesus is and what it really means to follow him. So like us! There have been flashes of insight quickly followed by statements that show they haven't got a clue (notably Mark 8:27–33). The disciples seem to struggle with spiritual blindness.

We conclude with the story of Bartimaeus who is presented as a model disciple. He responds to Jesus' call (v 49); he abandons his possessions (v 50), receives his sight and immediately follows Jesus along the road (which we now know leads to Jerusalem and the cross). All that Jesus has been trying to teach his disciples for months is modelled in a moment by Bartimaeus.

That's the way it is for some people: radical conversion, complete change of lifestyle, unhesitating obedience and no looking back. For many of us Christian discipleship is rather more complicated, and progress is more inconsistent, as it was for the twelve. But isn't it refreshing, and challenging, when we come across a Bartimaeus? Maybe we are guilty of over-complicating the Christian life. Maybe we need to recover that instinctively obedient response to the call of Jesus.

> 'Go,' said Jesus, 'your faith has healed you.' Immediately he received his sight and followed Jesus along the road.
>
> Mark 10:52

RESPOND

Pray: 'And Jesus, I have promised to serve you [thee] to the end; oh, give me grace to follow, my master and my friend' (John Ernest Bode, 1869).

Bible in a year: Ezekiel 30,31; Psalms 123–125

Rooted

Creating safe spaces for children and young people to explore who they are, why they matter and the difference Jesus makes.

The Rooted model starts where young people are at, seeking to provide space for them to grow and flourish in a safe and compassionate Christian community.

GET ROOTED: SU.ORG.UK/ROOTED

Hub Cards

Leader's Guide

Journals (10 pack)

The Psalms

Hundreds of books have been written on the Psalms: academic commentaries, devotional reflections, songbooks, prayerbooks and more. The Psalms have inspired poets, painters, preachers, embroiderers and musicians. Many book titles include the words 'praying' and 'psalms', so how can we learn about prayer as we read the Psalms?

Anticipate a conversation with God

The psalmists often directed their speech at God. It is OK to rant into his ear! But we need to talk *with* God rather than *to* him, to do more listening.

God always 'speaks' through the Psalms, but occasionally his spoken word is recorded. After Psalm 12's desperate cry, 'Help LORD ... those who are loyal have vanished from the human race' (v 1), God replies, 'Because the poor are plundered and the needy groan, I will now arise' (v 5).

Address God as a known person, not some vague divine being

Psalms provide a treasure trove of metaphors to use when speaking with God, to engage our imagination. There are titles to enrich our conversations with him,

one for every occasion: 'a shield around me' (3:3); 'fortress' and 'deliverer' (18:2); 'my light' (27:1); 'my Rock' (28:1); 'help in trouble' (46:1); 'hope' (71:5); 'Father' (89:26); 'Lord of all the earth' (97:5); lover of justice (99:4); 'the Maker of heaven and earth' (121:2); 'God of gods' (136:2); 'my God the King' (145:1).

Pray in various ways

Psalms were written over many centuries, from the reign of King David to the time of God's people's return from exile. We find more psalms of lament at the beginning of the psalter and more psalms of praise at the end. In the middle, Psalm 88, a lament, marks the darkest place.

Many psalms, however, begin in one form of prayer and move to another. For example, Psalm 32 includes penitence near the beginning, 'I will confess my transgressions to the LORD' (v 5), then moves to a prayer of thankfulness: 'Rejoice in the LORD and be glad' (v 11). Psalm 68 begins with a petition, 'May God arise, may his enemies be scattered' (v 1), but continues with praise, recalling what God has done: he 'sets the lonely in families' (v 6) and goes before his people in the wilderness (v 7).

Allow 'God's eyes' to shape our view of the world

Life experiences in the Old Testament are far removed from those of the twenty-first century. Yet we have in common the full range of emotions found in the Psalms – and God never changes. So we use Psalm 146 in modern prayer, knowing God seeks justice, upholding the cause of the oppressed, giving food to the hungry (v 7).

We may think that the bloodthirstiness in psalms like 137 (vs 7–9) or 139 (v 19) is unpleasantly archaic, even intrusive. But its presence is important. We must be able to express honest, angry emotions to God. His anger also rages at the horrors of sin. 'The LORD is a God who avenges ... pay back to the proud what they deserve' (Psalm 94:1,2).

Learn and use them when words fail, as Jesus did

Jesus heard and learned the Old Testament at his mother's knee. He must have used psalms in his prayers. At significant moments he quoted from them – when tempted (Psalm 91:11,12; Luke 4:9–11), when cleansing the Temple (Psalm 69:9; John 2:17), in debating with the chief priests (Psalm 110:1; Matthew 22:44; Psalm 118:22–24; Mark 12:10), and as he hung on the cross (Psalm 22:1; Mark 15:34; Psalm 31:5; Luke 23:46). These were the words that came to his mind in his agony.

Use individually and as a community, globally and across the ages

Some psalms, like Psalm 17, were prayers of individuals, yet could be spoken or sung by the whole congregation. Other psalms were clearly written to be sung by the community, such as Psalm 137 reflecting on the sorrows in exile and the joy of their return. Psalms in corporate worship enable us to join in solidarity with God's people before Christ, and with his body, the church, since Christ.

Psalms accompany us throughout life

In several books, Walter Brueggemann has suggested that psalms take us on a journey through our lives, from a state of orientation when all is well, through times of troubled disorientation – 'How long, LORD ... will you hide your face from me?' (13:1) – to ultimate reorientation with a deepened faith.

God's invitation is never absent. 'Taste and see that the LORD is good' (34:8).

Writer: Ro Willoughby

Further resources:
W Brueggemann, *Praying the Psalms*, Paternoster/Wipf and Stock, 2007
I Stackhouse, *Praying Psalms, A Personal Journey through the Psalter*, Wipf and Stock, 2018
M Guite, *David's Crown, Sounding the Psalms*, Canterbury Press, 2021

From long ago to eternity

About the writer
Mike Hawthorne

After many years of mission in Asia, Mike and his wife, Sue, have settled into a large, rambling old house in Herefordshire, which they use for various types of hospitality ministry.

If you are reading this I expect that, like me, you are peculiar: another anomaly of human history! I am guessing you share my sense that peace, security and a wide selection of breakfast cereals is somehow normal. Now I fear that we have been kidding ourselves. The majority of our race, through history and across the world today, endure lives much more like those described so graphically by the prophet Isaiah (probably in the later eighth century BC). This great writer enables us to appreciate how it would feel to live in a community where 'normal' has broken down, decency is a forlorn hope and powerful, wicked aggressors might at any time plunder our homes and drag our loved ones into slavery. We might find it easier to picture ancient Tyre or Jerusalem reduced to rubble. Isaiah would assert that there is nothing any more eternal about – say – modern Oxford or Paris.

The western society of my own days (since 1954) has been unusually blessed. Now it seems very possible that our grandchildren will confront threats as inevitable and unnavigable as those lived by Isaiah. The pandemic, terrible wars, the current cost of living crisis, movements of desperate migrants and many harbingers of a climate emergency suggest a near future in which humanity may reach the ends of our resources and of our wits. Will Isaiah chapter 29 verse 19 then be realised in our days? 'Once more the humble will rejoice in the LORD; the needy will rejoice in the Holy One of Israel.'

Fight for what's right?

PREPARE

These are dense, complex passages. Begin by reading this in a modern paraphrase, asking God to help you understand.

READ

Isaiah 22:1–25

EXPLORE

The 'Valley of Vision' is Jerusalem, the focal point for much of the prophetic energy in the Old Testament. It is a somewhat ironic name for the city in this chapter: a right *vision* is just what these Israelites seem to lack. Verses 1 to 3 outline a scene of flailing chaos. Revelry mixes with squalid, ignoble death. Note the two things *not* happening. No one is standing ready to fight for the city. And even later, as the enemy draws near, no one is turning to God for help (v 11b). The Lord does indeed have a word for them – see verse 12 – but to the corrupted hearts of the Israelites, this seems too hard a road to take (v 13).

Are we any different? Modern life aims to shield us from 'tumult and trampling and terror' – and can do quite a convincing job. It is, indeed, very difficult for most people to envisage threats and horrors to come, especially when food, wine and fun are (mostly) to be had right

now. Shebna, the steward of Jerusalem, may make us wonder whether God might be saying to our own leaders, 'What are you doing here?' Eliakim is a far better official. His name means 'God will raise up'. Even so, historically, this security will not last (v 25).

> The Lord, the LORD Almighty, has a day of tumult and trampling and terror in the Valley of Vision …
>
> Isaiah 22:5

RESPOND

Pray that God will raise up great and godly leaders for our own times.

Bible in a year: Ezekiel 32,33; 2 Peter 1

Nothing ungodly endures

PREPARE
Picture your favourite city. What do you love about it?

. . . .

READ
Isaiah 23:1–18

EXPLORE
Tyre was already ancient and famous in Isaiah's time. See Ezekiel chapter 27 for a detailed account of the glories of Tyre. Not everyone enjoys urban settings but there is no denying that, through history, they have been centres of much that is most civilised and wonderful in the world – or, at least, in the material world. It must have been inconceivable to the wealthy merchants of Tyre that, in their own time, their city would be reduced to rubble.

'Be silent' (v 2) is a grim command for a community whose heart should be the bustle and good cheer of prosperity. Verse 9 confirms that all this activity and worldly achievement is of little account to God. Modern social scientists remind us that many aspects of modern cities are no more permanent or reliable. The New York stock exchange; the London property market; the overcrowding and pollution in Delhi and Dhaka: none of these is established on the eternal values of God's kingdom.

Tyre is still there today. It has endured years of war and foreign invasions. According to the United Nations, approximately a third of the population are refugees living in three main camps. In the Tyre urban area, 43 per cent of Lebanese are living in poverty. Food insecurity has become a major issue. Don't let anyone tell you that Old Testament prophecy isn't relevant.

The LORD Almighty planned it, to bring down her pride in all her splendour and to humble all who are renowned on the earth.
Isaiah 23:9

RESPOND
God understands how to plan cities. Read Revelation chapter 21 verses 2 and 22 to 27 and praise his name.

. . . .

Bible in a year: Ezekiel 34,35; 2 Peter 2

Ain't seen nothing yet

PREPARE

Pray for those parts of the world suffering the devastating effects of climate change.

READ

Isaiah 24:1–23

EXPLORE

A prophet's job is to speak the mind of God. We must not be surprised, then, if in Isaiah we read words which seem to come both from and for eternity. These sections of scripture are sometimes called 'The Isaiah Apocalypse'. This word means 'unveiling of the end'. Isaiah has access to divine realities. These might be beyond our comprehension and we should not pretend otherwise. However, as image piles upon ghastly image, it is clear that the end will be terrible.

I prayed before I began writing this note: how to find something helpful to say about the catastrophic destruction of the world?! My first sense as I prayed was of how tiny I am. This is true in terms of the time as well as the space I occupy. Mixed in with all the horror, without any signal to the reader, are verses 14 to 16a and verse 23. At first, this seems strange. Surely the idea is not of a group comprising you, me, our Christian chums and a few righteous Israelites, all celebrating while the rest of the world suffers anguish. If we think this, we are mistakenly reading the chapter like a modern, ordered narrative. Instead, here we are being given a glimpse of God's intention through all time: righteous judgement but also glory in which we may share.

From the ends of the earth we hear singing: 'Glory to the Righteous One.'

Isaiah 24:16

RESPOND

List some of the world's current problems and then pray (or sing), 'Glory to the Righteous One.'

Bible in a year: Ezekiel 36,37; Psalms 126–128

The beauty of law

PREPARE

How many words can you think of that mean something like 'law'? Look in a thesaurus if you like.

READ

Psalm 119:49–72

EXPLORE

People, in our muddled way, sometimes seem to proceed as if there are two Gods. There's a nice one, who is all about grace, love and forgiveness. Then there's the scary one, who deals in laws, judgement and wrath. Christians are not exempt from this sort of theological confusion. The truth, of course, is that there is one God and that, through Jesus' accomplishment on the cross, we may come to experience the first set of divine attributes and can thankfully escape the consequences of the second.

However, both the book of Isaiah and the psalms testify that reality is not as simple as all that. The astonishing theme of Psalm 119 is that there is hope, comfort and rejoicing to be found not only in God's loving kindness but also in his law. Perhaps this is hard for someone in our age to fully grasp. I might check the planning laws or the Highway Code to find out what I ought to do. As a

Christian, I might search the Scriptures for guidance on how my church or my family should behave. The psalmist mentions 'the law' in almost every verse (using various vocabulary) but he does not once mention any rules he should obey. Instead, the law is his delight (v 70). Could we be missing something here?

> The law from your mouth is more precious to me than thousands of pieces of silver and gold.
>
> Psalm 119:72

RESPOND

Praise the Lord because, ultimately, our lives are ordered by him, and not subject to the chaos of wickedness.

Bible in a year: Ezekiel 38,39; 2 Peter 3

God picks up the bill

PREPARE

The Lord has prepared a banquet for you. What exactly is on the menu?

READ

Isaiah 25:1–12

EXPLORE

The central point of this chapter is the great feast which the Lord has prepared (v 6). Notice that the table is spread 'for all peoples'. Remember that this is apocalyptic writing, akin to the final passages in Revelation. Verses 7 and 8 wonderfully describe an ultimate event through which God will destroy all that is dark, wicked and deathly. What, I wonder, is 'the shroud that enfolds all peoples'? Perhaps it's our spiritual blindness – or just that grey, sad feeling which so many people pass through life with. Now gone for ever, praise be to God.

There are two songs here. The first – verses 1 to 8 – is by an individual, presumably Isaiah. The second – from verse 9 – is a group of people celebrating their God. Both recount 'wonderful things' (v 1): God in action utterly destroying 'the ruthless' and saving and blessing his people. If you didn't know the very special God who has made all this happen, you would probably be surprised by verse 4. Amid cataclysmic events, we find God taking gentle care to ensure that the poor and the needy are sheltered and protected. Let us not doubt that such people have special servings reserved at the feast (v 6)!

> ... the LORD Almighty will prepare a feast of rich food for all peoples, a banquet of aged wine – the best of meats and the finest of wines.
>
> Isaiah 25:6

RESPOND

This is a word for all time. However, the people praising God here recount things he has achieved in their days. As you respond, praise God for what he has done specifically in our own age.

Bible in a year: Ezekiel 40,41; 1 John 1

Through turmoil to peace

PREPARE
Pray for a God's-eye perspective: that we might rise above our day-to-day worries.

READ
Isaiah 26:1–21

EXPLORE
At points this chapter feels just like a psalm giving glory to God (eg v 9); at others (eg vs 20,21) we receive the full blast of God's power and wrath. Again, we modern Christians are reminded that the same God can be at once terrifying and our trusted friend. Notice how frequently the material world is stirred in with the spiritual realm. Whether these gates, cities, footsteps and pathways are literal or symbolic is surely not the most important thing. However, a key in grasping the significance for us of these verses is the lead-in phrase: 'In that day'. Isaiah has in mind a time – or, perhaps more accurately, an eternal reality. In that day, the Lord will have finally resolved all the struggles of both ancient Israel and the twenty-first century.

We can glean remarkable details here about God's coming and for ever kingdom. It is strong, yes, but why? Because of his salvation! The city is at peace, because those who dwell there have minds fixed for ever on the Lord. Isaiah is a realist. As many harrowing images show us, he is fully engaged with the pain and turmoil of the times in which he lives. He is also a godly prophet: he can readily envisage the ultimate victory for which he waits. And so, his mind is steadfast (v 3).

> You will keep in perfect peace those whose minds are steadfast, because they trust in you.
>
> Isaiah 26:3

RESPOND
Verse 8 describes people waiting for God: 'we wait for you'. Set aside some time to do this yourself.

Bible in a year: Ezekiel 42,43; 1 John 2

With God to the summit

PREPARE

In verse 5 of today's passage, God says, '... let them make peace with me'. How should the Israelites go about this?

READ

Isaiah 27:1–13

EXPLORE

Sometimes Isaiah seems to be all over the place! I mean two things. First, my modern mind likes linear outlines and logical connections: it's challenging at times to follow Isaiah's thinking. People saw things very differently so long ago. Secondly, the genius of Isaiah (or, should I say, of the Holy Spirit?) is to focus sharply on a specific time and place while at the same time describing realities far beyond the struggling Israelites of the late eighth century. We are 'in that day' again. We might leave the question of *when* that day will be to God. However, Isaiah does give us various pointers as to its nature and context.

Deliverance is the central theme. First Leviathan, the representative huge, evil entity, is defeated (v 1). Then a range of horticultural images are used to present God's longing to save, nurture and nourish his people. Verse 4 is a distinctive expression of God's heart, and in verse 12 it is the Lord himself who gathers in the harvest. It is not an easy process. We sense here something of the struggle which God has set himself to bring people back to his 'holy mountain' (v 13). To achieve this by force would be simple for him. He has resolved to accomplish his divine purpose through love.

And in that day a great trumpet will sound. Those who were perishing in Assyria and those who were exiled in Egypt will come and worship the LORD on the holy mountain in Jerusalem.

Isaiah 27:13

RESPOND

Imagine yourself climbing the holy mountain. What do you pray as you climb?

Bible in a year: Ezekiel 44,45; Psalms 129–131

Urban decay writ large

PREPARE
What do you think might be the key differences between your home and a settlement in ancient Israel?

READ
Isaiah 28:1–29

EXPLORE
Ephraim (vs 1–13) refers to the northern part of Israel with its once beautiful capital at Samaria. Jerusalem was the capital of the southern kingdom of Judah. Here, Isaiah describes two decadent, corrupted societies. Upon both, God turns his terrifying, righteous eye of judgement. Disgusting drunkenness seems to be an obvious feature (vs 7,8), but behind these we can also discern undeserved pride and outrageous arrogance. Like many residents of modern cities, they fool themselves that the consequences of wickedness will pass them by (v 15). What's striking is that the groups singled out for special condemnation are not the thieves and prostitutes, but priests and prophets! Verses 10 and 13 suggest that God's Word is dismissed and mocked by spiritual leaders. These rulers are called 'scoffers' (v 14): an especially low form of insult in Old Testament thought.

This is tragic because what their Lord is offering is so lovely, so wholly desirable in comparison with the embattled, shrivelling communities in which the Israelites are just about hanging on. God's Word in verse 12 is key: 'This is rest.' It's the same idea as was ultimately promised to Abraham when he set out for the Promised Land. Notice who is offering – still! – to do all the work. In verse 16, God himself is laying solid, 'precious' foundations. All his people are asked to do is believe.

> ... the Sovereign LORD says: 'See, I lay a stone in Zion, a tested stone, a precious cornerstone for a sure foundation ...'
>
> Isaiah 28:16

RESPOND
Pray that justice and righteousness will be restored to your own nation.

Bible in a year: Ezekiel 46,47; 1 John 3

God arrives: be afraid

PREPARE
What does the word 'woe' mean to you?

READ
Isaiah 29:1–24

EXPLORE

Jerusalem (with the code name here of Ariel) was intended as the spiritual heart of the kingdom. Now, grimly, Isaiah is letting us know that God has decided to burn up Jerusalem so that nothing is left except – as it were – ashes on a hearth. As in much of Isaiah, the chapter predicts two waves of catastrophe sweeping over Israel. The more superficial assault comes from worldly enemies: Assyria, Babylon and so on. Bad enough, but the second and more dreadful attack comes from God himself, as he turns almighty wrath upon his faithless people. How would our own nations measure up? Confronted with existential disaster, the Israelites appear as neither terrified nor repentant nor fighting for their lives. Rather they seem, in verses 9 to 12, to be vaguely addled. The books of Samuel and Kings recount how God's people slowly lost their ability to comprehend God's Word, even as their worldly kingdom declined and then fell.

Today's passage ends on a note of ultimate hope. We may allow ourselves an ironic smile as, in verse 17, the scripture offers us a God's-eye perspective, referring to 'a very short time'. It is likely that verses 17 to 24 describe the very end of time! The promise is no less true and no less wonderful for all that.

The Lord says: 'These people come near to me with their mouth and honour me with their lips, but their hearts are far from me ...'
Isaiah 29:13

RESPOND
Pray for the community in which you live, that it will be protected from the diverse catastrophes that befall lovely places.

Bible in a year: Ezekiel 48; 1 John 4

Glimpses of goodness

PREPARE
What sorts of behaviour do you believe make God most angry? Make a list.

....

READ
Isaiah 30:1–18

EXPLORE
We can compile a long list, from today's passage, of human attitudes and behaviours that make God angry. Obstinacy comes first, followed by those who make their own plans. Wrong relationships and agreements are a bad idea – those not led by the Holy Spirit. Assuming that Egypt, or your insurance company, will keep you safe is another silly notion (v 2). Dealings with dodgy officials (vs 4,5) might suggest that we would be well advised to choose ethical investment banks and advisers. The second section (vs 6–11) is a warning to any age that chooses not to listen to God's Word and, instead, chooses to heed the voices they want to hear. What might these voices be in our times, I wonder?

And then, central in this reading is the loveliness of verses 15, 18 and 19. This seems to be a motif in Isaiah – even in the Old Testament as a whole: wonderful nuggets of reassuring truth and blessing are inserted between longer sections of desolation and misery. What are we to make of this general pattern? I wonder whether we can understand the majority of the sections as a reasonable, balanced, God's-eye perspective on the human story. Then perhaps the beautiful, uplifting promises are like those special insights that Christians are given unexpectedly – of the love and goodness of our Lord.

> Yet the LORD longs to be gracious to you; therefore he will rise up to show you compassion. For the LORD is a God of justice. Blessed are all who wait for him!
>
> Isaiah 30:18

RESPOND
Read verse 18 again. Meditate on God's compassion and justice.

....

Bible in a year: Daniel 1–3; Psalms 132–134

Longing for God

PREPARE

What sort of person do you think God sees when he looks at you – not in terms of holiness and wickedness but concerning more specific personality traits that you feel are important to him?

READ

Psalm 119:73–96

EXPLORE

We discover a lot today, from the writing, about the person responsible for Psalm 119. The first quality we may notice is a special intimacy with God which is evident through these verses. There is no suggestion of a stereotypical 'Old Testament' approach via temple and sacrifice. Body, mind and spirit – the writer seems engaged with someone with whom he has an open, unshakeable relationship. The entire section is addressed to God himself (this varies through the psalms). The writer is sure that at the heart of the relationship is the love God constantly shows him (v 76).

Like a modern Christian, the psalmist hopes that the demonstration of his faith will draw others to God (vs 74,79). This is perhaps more in hope than in expectation: the circumstances of the writer are not obvious, but it is clear that they involve real persecution and a serious threat to his life (vs 78,84–88). There seems to be a difference between the expressions of faith in the first section (vs 73–80) and in the the last (vs 89–96). In the verses headed 'Yodh', we sense someone experiencing the very presence of God. In the later verses, headed 'Lamedh', perhaps the feeling of God's actual company has faded. The writer needs to recall, by faith, the truth of God's Word.

My soul faints with longing for your salvation, but I have put my hope in your word.

Psalm 119:81

RESPOND

Ask the Holy Spirit for that same sense of intense longing for him.

Bible in a year: Daniel 4,5; 1 John 5

The urgency of God

PREPARE
As you prepare, imagine God hurrying to be with you, as you 'wait' for him (v 18).

. . . .

READ
Isaiah 30:19–33

EXPLORE
Verse 18 (from Saturday's passage) provides a key overlapping point with today's verses. After much feverish activity from others, God 'rises'. This feels like a full, New Testament revelation of his nature. At the heart of it are grace, compassion and justice. Because of these, we can see in verse 19 the same loving father who runs delightedly towards the prodigal son (see Luke 15:20).

All we can expect from God is well encompassed here in these verses. As his people, when we cry for help we can look for his immediate response (v 19), his intimate presence (v 21) and his bountiful provision (vs 23–25). By now, I guess, we are ready for Isaiah's lurch in verse 25 – from broad, tranquil meadows, through horrible slaughter, and back to streams of water and gentle healing (v 26).

Finally, we plunge back into destruction, the raging anger of God's judgement and fire pits. (Topheth is something like an ancient cremation place, verse 33.) Yet still – mixed in a way that's strange to our modern sensibilities – are images of holy festivity, rejoicing and celebration (v 29). Isaiah's God-given vision shows realities which we know must come to pass. God will destroy all that is wicked. He will restore his kingdom – and then invite us in.

> And you will sing as on the night you celebrate a holy festival; your hearts will rejoice as when people playing pipes go up to the mountain of the LORD, to the Rock of Israel.
>
> Isaiah 30:29

RESPOND
Just now, what are the bruises you carry from life? Ask the Lord to bind them up right now (v 26).

. . . .

Bible in a year: Daniel 6,7; 2 John

Seeds of salvation

Isn't it amazing how relevant and immediate parts of the ancient Hebrew, Greek and Aramaic texts we now know as the Bible can feel? It is nice to have commentaries and expositors on hand, but it doesn't take a scholar to tell us what a verse like, 'Love your enemies and pray for those who persecute you' (Matthew 5:44) means.

But then there are those parts like Isaiah 31 to 39... a whole other story! We have to stretch our minds and imaginations to inhabit a society where lives were often short and bloody, kingdoms small, vulnerable and unstable, little god-statues all over the place – worshipped in a desperate attempt to overcome impossible odds.

In this time and place, God was at work. He was speaking. He was calling a people to declare his glory, power, love and mercy so that the whole world might know him. In this stony, weedy, dusty ground, he planted seeds of salvation. Through Jesus, salvation has come.

As we read of how, yet again, the people of Israel chose not to trust God, faced God-sanctioned onslaught from a stronger enemy force, ignored their prophet and succumbed to pride, let's marvel at God's astonishing faithfulness through generations and his awesome ability to bring his purposes to pass regardless of humankind's ability to mess up.

The zeal of the Lord has indeed accomplished this (Isaiah 37:32).

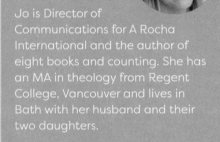

About the writer
Jo Swinney

Jo is Director of Communications for A Rocha International and the author of eight books and counting. She has an MA in theology from Regent College, Vancouver and lives in Bath with her husband and their two daughters.

Trust and obey

PREPARE

Today's reading speaks of God hovering like a bird over Jerusalem, shielding it with his wings. Picture yourself sheltered under the wings of the Lord Almighty, protected from all harm. Let him quieten your fears.

READ

Isaiah 31:1–9

EXPLORE

A small, beleaguered nation faces a far stronger enemy and turns to a neighbour for help. Egypt has a multitude of chariots, horses and muscle-bound horsemen. An alliance would give the Israelites a fighting chance of survival. Horses, chariots and strong men seem like a safe bet. They can be experienced through the five senses. They seem a good match for the scale of the threat. What could be wrong about that?

What is wrong is that Israel is choosing Egypt over God (vs 1,6). In trusting Egypt they are explicitly disbelieving that divine power can defeat the strength of 'mere mortals' (v 3) and disobeying God's clear and very specific instruction that they never return to Egypt for horses (Deuteronomy 17:16).

The lesson from this historical episode is not that we must choose between

taking out an insurance policy and trusting God. Or that nations shouldn't form alliances as they did in the First and Second World Wars. Trusting God means obeying him on those things he has made clear to us, including discarding idolatry (31:7), regardless of whether we want to or understand his reasoning.

> Woe to those who go down to Egypt for help … but do not look to the Holy One of Israel, or seek help from the LORD.
>
> Isaiah 31:1

RESPOND

Where in your life are you knowingly disregarding God's commands because you think there is a better way to handle things? What would it look like to *really* trust him?

Bible in a year: Daniel 8,9; 3 John

I love you, tomorrow

PREPARE
Take two minutes to sit in silence before the Lord. He may speak to you, or he may not, but he is with you.

READ
Isaiah 32:1–20

EXPLORE
In the northern hemisphere, winter has now properly taken hold. Many trees are entirely bare, their branches dead-looking wooden sticks; birds and insects are quiet and hidden. It is hard to conceive of the landscape in its full springtime glory, but the seasons continue to cycle.

There's a cycle here too – sin, suffering, repentance and rescue, then back to sinning. The wealthy women of Jerusalem seem to have forgotten what follows sin and they've become complacent. Assyria was about to devastate their land – there was time to react if they had only paid attention, but they continued to happily swan about in their finery, blithely ignoring the troublesome prophet.

At its worst, Judah must have seemed as dead as a tree in midwinter. How could life ever return? What hope of renewal could there be? The hope then, as now, rests on the shoulders of the righteous king (v 1). Jesus came to announce his kingdom and one day he will return to bring peace: 'quietness and confidence for ever' (v 17) for people and the rest of creation. Our task is to live in full acceptance of the painful reality that is today, doing what we can to get ready for a better tomorrow.

> The fruit of that righteousness will be peace; its effect will be quietness and confidence for ever.
>
> Isaiah 32:17

RESPOND
Is there any danger about which you are being complacent? Ask God to give you the courage to face it head on. He won't let you be crushed.

Bible in a year: Daniel 10–12; Psalms 135,136

The power of one

PREPARE

Leading a country is a phenomenal responsibility. Pray for the leaders of the government where you are and any others who come to mind.

READ

Isaiah 33:1–24

EXPLORE

My husband is an Anglican vicar. The selection process for his current church included an interview with a panel of five, a grilling from a group of children from the church primary school, a lunch with staff and key leaders, a dinner with the PCC (which is like a board of trustees) and meetings with several groups of church members. That might seem rather extreme, but people understand how important it is to choose their leader wisely. A bad leader can do untold damage, as the roster of Israel's and Judah's kings so clearly illustrates.

Today's reading gives us a clear sense of what kind of ruler we have in the Lord God and the society that will flourish under his leadership. The Lord reigns with justice and righteousness (v 5), power that keeps enemies at bay (v 3), as judge, lawmaker and saviour (v 22). In the truest, deepest sense, he is beautiful (v 17). With him as king, there is stability (v 6), reliable provision of food, water and shelter (vs 16,20,23) and peace with God, people and the land.

As Christians, we have declared allegiance to this king. And one day every knee will bow to him. Come, Lord Jesus. We long for you (v 2).

> For the LORD is our judge, the LORD is our lawgiver, the LORD is our king; it is he who will save us.
>
> Isaiah 33:22

RESPOND

Choose one or two attributes of God highlighted in this passage and contemplate them with a worshipful heart.

Bible in a year: Hosea 1,2; Jude

The whole earth groans

PREPARE

This passage has many references to owls (vs 11,13,15). Ask God to give you a glimpse of how he sees these beautiful birds.

READ

Isaiah 34:1–17

Edom's animosity towards the people of God began with the conflict of Jacob and Esau, settling into a hardened pattern of hostility by Numbers 20:14–21. Gruesome as the retribution they face may be, there is just cause. Why then is the soil (v 7), water (v 9) and air (v 10) polluted and defiled? Why all the animal slaughter (vs 6,7a)?

First of all, there are clues here directing us to see Edom as a stand-in, a motif for something of a different scale (v 5). This is judgement relating to nations, individuals, the environment, the entire cosmos (vs 1–4). In his holiness, God has no tolerance for sin. And it is human sin that is the greatest cause of suffering to the earth and its inhabitants. Gus Speth, former US adviser on climate, said: 'I used to think that the top environmental problems were biodiversity loss, ecosystem collapse and climate change. I was wrong. The top environmental problems are selfishness, greed and apathy. To deal with these, we need a cultural and spiritual transformation.'*

God has good plans for redemption and restoration for the whole of his creation (Romans 8:21,22). As his Spirit works transformation in us, one of the results will be that we become a blessing not a curse to the earth.

Desert creatures will meet with hyenas, and wild goats will bleat to each other; there the night creatures will also lie down and find for themselves places of rest.

Isaiah 34:14

RESPOND

Spend time in repentance for the ways in which your selfishness, greed and apathy have harmed creation.

*https://tinyurl.com/mr4cu8rc

Bible in a year: Hosea 3–6; Revelation 1

A homebound highway

PREPARE

Pray: 'Open my eyes and unstop my ears, Lord, so I can see and hear you clearly today. Amen.'

READ

Isaiah 35:1–10

EXPLORE

The people of Israel were very familiar with long journeys through deserts. First Abram, then Isaac, then Jacob and Joseph. The exodus was a 40-year trek and the forced march to Babylon a shorter but far nastier few weeks. The desert meant exposure to extreme temperatures and the fear and discomfort of insufficient food and water sources. We may not have experienced literal deserts, but all of us have lived in desert times where hope has scant soil in which to grow.

In this beautiful poem, the dusty trudge becomes a pilgrimage, the wayside gloriously decked out in joyful expression of the splendour of God (v 2). There are several ways in which the traveller is strengthened: first, by seeing the signs of God's presence and love all around (vs 5–7); secondly, holding on to the truth that God is coming to save (v 4); and thirdly, by staying on the Way of Holiness which leads to everlasting joy (vs 8,10).

We are not wandering directionless through life until we stumble upon a meaningless death. We are on a highway to home. We are not alone on our journey; we are among a great throng of fellow believers and accompanied by the Lord God himself.

> And a highway will be there; it will be called the Way of Holiness; it will be for those who walk on that Way.
>
> Isaiah 35:8

RESPOND

The imperative in verse 4 is to encourage the fearful with the words, 'Be strong, do not fear; your God will come'. Who might you say that to? Do you need to say it to yourself?

Bible in a year: Hosea 7,8; Psalms 137,138

A guidebook for the ages

PREPARE

Bring to mind a significant decision you have made lately. In what ways did you seek God's will and how did he speak to you?

READ

Psalm 119:97–112

EXPLORE

Yesterday evening I went for a night walk with my daughter. Most of our route was lit by streetlights but for a short stretch we were in pitch darkness. I couldn't even see my own feet. It would have been easy to trip over, take a wrong turn or step on our black cat who had come along for the walk.

Isaiah refers to 'people walking in darkness' (9:2), by which he means those who live beyond God's blazing light of love and life. Much later, John's Gospel identifies Jesus as 'the light of all mankind' (1:4), and Paul in his letter to the Galatians urges people to be led by the Spirit. Here in Psalm 119, another central means of God's guidance to us is celebrated: his Word, the Bible. The light it shines on our path is wisdom, insight and understanding (vs 98–100) and the ability to discern between good and evil behaviour (vs 101,104).

There is absolutely no need for us to stumble around trying to figure out the way ahead. If we meditate on, memorise and practise what we read in God's Word, we have all we need to set our course in a godly direction.

Your word is a lamp for my feet, a light on my path.
Psalm 119:105

RESPOND

Pray: "'Accept, LORD, the willing praise of my mouth, and teach me your laws" (v 108). Amen.'

Bible in a year: Hosea 9,10; Revelation 2

Back at the aqueduct

PREPARE

There is nothing we can't say to God. Tell him – truthfully – what is on your mind.

• •

READ

Isaiah 36:1–22

EXPLORE

Assyria has swept through Judah, capturing city after city, and the army arrives at the walls of Jerusalem riding high on their victories. Representing King Sennacherib, the field commander meets King Hezekiah's spokesmen at the same aqueduct where Isaiah had confronted a defiant King Ahaz (Isaiah 7:3,10–13).

Seeds of disobedience have grown and borne bitter fruit. As the field commander puts it with scathing wit, leaning on Egypt was only going to give them splinters (v 6), there was a reasonable chance they would have to eat their own excrement, and God was not going to bail them out this time (vs 12–15)!

It was always God's intention that in choosing one nation to be his own, that nation would be a beacon for others. Assyria is in many ways a terrible, godless nation, but here we see it claiming to enact the will of the Lord (36:10). The Assyrians can see this God has high standards for his people and that there are consequences for them in disobeying him. But Assyria will pay the price for its blasphemy (vs 19,20). In all this, God's power and glory will be displayed, giving multitudes the chance to respond in righteous fear and worship.

> '… have I come to attack and destroy this land without the LORD? The LORD himself told me to march against this country and destroy it.'
>
> Isaiah 36:4,10

RESPOND

What are today's headlines? Pray for those caught up in each situation, that they would have eyes to see how God is at work to bring about his good purposes.

• •

Bible in a year: Hosea 11,12; Revelation 3

Distress and disgrace

PREPARE

How do you feel when you hear Jesus made fun of or insulted? Take a few moments to analyse your feelings and what they show you about how you see God.

···

READ

Isaiah 37:1–20

EXPLORE

The field commander has touched a nerve, not by threatening death and destruction but by mocking the living God. Hezekiah can't bear it. He carries out the symbolic gesture of ripping up his finery and replacing it with sackcloth, sends emissaries to the prophet Isaiah with a pleading message and heads to the Temple to pray (vs 14–20). It is unbearable to think that God will allow his name to sit alongside those of wood and stone gods carved by people.

The blasphemous ridicule has cleared Hezekiah's mind. He has not always shown God the respect, honour and worship he deserves, but in this moment, he understands: 'You alone are God over all the kingdoms of the earth. You have made heaven and earth' (37:16).

The field commander won't get away with his disrespect, but many people do – at least in the short term. Even the mockers around Jesus' cross didn't seem to suffer consequences. Jesus told us that following him would mean being treated in the same ways he was. And that one day vindication would come 'so that all the kingdoms of the earth may know that' the Lord is the only God (37:20).

> … 'This is what Hezekiah says: this day is a day of distress and rebuke and disgrace, as when children come to the moment of birth and there is no strength to deliver them.'
>
> Isaiah 37:3

RESPOND

Pray for those who misjudge the living God, that they would repent before it is too late.

···

Bible in a year: Hosea 13,14; Revelation 4

A harvest of hope

PREPARE
When we come to the end of ourselves and find God is all we have, he is enough. Ask the Holy Spirit to enable you to believe this is true.

READ
Isaiah 37:21–38

EXPLORE
There are walled cities all around the world. They were designed with the security of their inhabitants in mind. They have slits in the ramparts through which weapons can be fired against the enemy, who are kept from the citizens within by impenetrable barriers of rock.

The problem was that all an attacking army needed to do to achieve victory was camp out long enough for the food in the city to run out. The Assyrians not only had Jerusalem under siege, but they had also created conditions for a famine on a far larger scale by confiscating the crops ready in March and April and preventing the farmers from sowing in September and October. If they weren't to die of starvation, surely their only option was to submit to Assyria (2 Chronicles 32:11)?

God is not going to let that happen. Through Isaiah, Hezekiah learns that there will be a harvest of food that has planted itself (v 30). A remnant of his people will come through this horrific situation, taking root and bearing fruit (vs 31,32). In some sense, we, citizens of God's kingdom in the twenty-first century, are their fruit. The Lord Almighty will always accomplish what he says he will.

'... This year you will eat what grows by itself, and the second year what springs from that. But in the third year sow and reap, plant vineyards and eat their fruit.'
Isaiah 37:30

RESPOND
Are you under siege and in need of a miracle? Take heart! Your God can do more than you could ask or imagine.

Bible in a year: Joel 1,2; Psalm 139

Extension granted

PREPARE
What items sit at the top of your to-do list right now? Prayerfully reflect on whether you have prioritised the right things.

READ
Isaiah 38:1-22

EXPLORE
One of the most perplexing questions in life is why God allows some people to suffer and die while others experience his miraculous intervention. Seldom do we get even a glimpse of the divine purposes at work.

But in Hezekiah's case, we can take an educated guess. As a king in a lineage notable for its horrific idolatry, pagan practices and God-shaming leadership, Hezekiah stands out for his – albeit patchy – record of devotion and doing what is good in God's eyes (38:3). His father, Ahaz (2 Chronicles 28:1-4), and his son, Manasseh (2 Chronicles 33:1-6), were complete and utter blighters. In giving him an additional 15 years (vs 4-6), God is extending the period during which his wrath is not incurred, and all can live in the light of his favour. 2 Chronicles 32:26-33 records this as an era of peace, prosperity and spiritual devotion.

It is quite understandable that we plead with God to extend our lives and those of our loved ones. Sometimes he will grant an extension; often he won't. All we can do is accept his gift of time, however much of it we are given, and use it as well as we can.

'Go and tell Hezekiah, "This is what the LORD, the God of your father David, says: I have heard your prayer and seen your tears; I will add fifteen years to your life."'

Isaiah 38:5

RESPOND
The Westminster Shorter Catechism says, 'Man's chief end is to glorify God, and to enjoy him for ever.' How does this line up with how you see your life's main purpose?

Bible in a year: Joel 3; Revelation 5

Dangers of sunlit uplands

PREPARE

'Speak, Lord, for your servant is listening' (1 Samuel 3:9).

· ·

READ

Isaiah 39:1–8

EXPLORE

On his deathbed, weak, vulnerable and diminished (chapter 38), Hezekiah was spiritually far stronger than we find him in chapter 39. News of his miraculous recovery had prompted a state visit, accompanied by gifts and no doubt a generous helping of flattery (v 1). Babylon's ascendancy was in the future. Hezekiah's guard was down, and he gave away valuable information about his people's assets for the simple and basic pleasure of showing off (v 2). Isaiah is left to tell him the scope of his error: Babylon will one day take all the treasures of the kingdom and his descendants into exile (vs 5–7).

1 Peter 5:8 says, 'Be alert and of sober mind. Your enemy the devil prowls around like a roaring lion looking for someone to devour.' Our enemy is the master of disguise and knows better than to prance around with a pitchfork and flashing red eyes, advertising his presence. We need to get wise to his tactics, one of which is to attack when we are most complacent and comfortable, as we can see he did in today's reading (v 8). There is a reason the church often flourishes under persecution: everyone knows how very badly they need the Lord. We don't need to make ourselves suffer to grow in spiritual strength and maturity, but we should be mindful that it takes extra effort when life is good.

> '… the time will surely come when everything in your palace, and all that your predecessors have stored up until this day, will be carried off to Babylon …'
>
> Isaiah 39:6

RESPOND

Consider where you might be most vulnerable to the devil's trouble-making and pray for God's protection.

· ·

Bible in a year: Amos 1,2; Revelation 6

Scripture Union

REVEALING JESUS

FREE:
- COACHING
- AMAZING RESOURCES
- ADVICE & SUPPORT

A flexible and FREE mission framework from Scripture Union

Helping you journey into faith with children and young people who aren't in church.

SU.ORG.UK/REVEALINGJESUS

Light and love for life

The apostle John was Jesus' closest friend. The years had passed, and the other disciples had all been killed. Now the elderly John was in his final years before joining Jesus and the original gang of disciples in heaven. In these latter years, traditionally, he is thought to have been the author of five books: his beautiful account of the life and ministry of Jesus, John's Gospel; the vision from Jesus that we call the book of Revelation; and these three letters.

John wrote to believers in churches that he knew well. His first letter is to believers hurting from a church split. A group had pulled out of the church to pursue their elite super-spiritual alternative. That group had been critical of those who remained and what they believed. Actually, in John's thinking this other group was not Christian at all (1 John 1:5–10). John wrote to reassure the believers that they already had the light and love that God had revealed in the person of Jesus Christ.

John wrote to two friends in the much shorter second and third letters. One was helping a church where truth was being compromised in the name of love, resulting in the church being vulnerable to travelling false teachers. The other was a church leader who hosted travelling teachers but faced difficulty from a dominant personality within the church.

John wrote in his typically simple wording that carries rich spiritual wisdom for the thoughtful reader. Let's live in God's light and love (1 John 1:6; 1 John 4:15,16).

About the writer
Peter Mead

Peter is one of the pastors at Trinity Chippenham and a mentor with Cor Deo. He teaches at Union School of Theology and at the European Leadership Forum. He has written several books, including *Pleased to Dwell* and *Lost in Wonder* (both with Christian Focus). He is married to Melanie.

The greatest privilege!

PREPARE

Take a moment to consider each of your senses. What can you see? Do you hear anything? What about smell? The physical is important as well as the spiritual.

READ

1 John 1:1–4

EXPLORE

In John's time, some people struggled with the idea that Jesus had actually come in the flesh. They felt that this physical realm should be shunned and that Jesus must have existed only in a higher spiritual realm. John wanted them to know that Jesus had literally and physically lived among them (vs 2,3). The disciples had seen him, heard his voice and touched him. But his goal was not to show off his own experience. John wanted his readers to know they were invited to enjoy the greatest privilege.

The books of the New Testament are not a set of ancient myths. They are eyewitness accounts of actual history. That history tells of God's Son, Jesus, coming to earth and becoming one of us.

Why did Jesus come? There are two reasons: first, he came on a revelation mission. He came to let us discover what God is like as he showed the wonder of the relationship between God the Father and God the Son (v 2). Secondly, he came on a relational mission. He came to invite us to join in the glorious fellowship of the Trinity (v 3). The truth of that invitation is more real than anything we can see or touch today!

We proclaim to you what we have seen and heard, so that you also may have fellowship with us. And our fellowship is with the Father and with his Son, Jesus Christ.

1 John 1:3

RESPOND

How might the coming of Jesus 2,000 years ago affect your life today?

Bible in a year: Amos 3,4; Psalms 140,141

Mixed messages

PREPARE

Who speaks to you each week? Think about the people in your daily life: the preacher at church, the salesperson in the shop, the television and the radio. How many different messages do you hear every week?

READ

Psalm 119:113–128

EXPLORE

In these two sections of Psalm 119, the writer contrasts the words of the world with the Word of God. Ever since the serpent questioned God's Word in Genesis 3, we have lived in this war of words. The big question remains: who will we listen to, God or the enemy?

The psalmist recognises the problem. The words of the world are set against the Word of God. So he can say he hates double-minded people (v 113) and every wrong path (v 128). However, he loves God's law (v 113) and God's commands (v 127). He is clear that God is his refuge (v 114), the one who sustains him (vs 116,117), the one who loves him (v 124), and the one who will vindicate him (v 126).

The writer is clear that there is a contrast between the words of God and the words of the world. And yet, he asks for discernment from God, his teacher (vs 124,125). How many messages do we hear each week without questioning their validity?

> I am your servant; give me discernment that I may understand your statutes.
>
> **Psalm 119:125**

RESPOND

Pray: 'Loving God, my teacher, please grow greater discernment in me so that I can see through the messages coming at me from this world. I want to be more confident in your perfect instruction. Amen.'

Bible in a year: Amos 5,6; Revelation 7

God's cleaning project

PREPARE

What would you discover if you were to shine a torch into your attic, or cellar, or behind some old furniture? Perfect cleanliness – or might the light's beam find some dirt?

READ

1 John 1:5 – 2:2

EXPLORE

In this letter, John offers the life of God through two great truths: God is light (1:5) and God is love (4:8).

The light of God shines into our lives and will increasingly show up the dirty recesses of our inner reality. It would be inconsistent, and therefore wrong, to claim to be in fellowship with God but actually to live in darkness (1:6). Yet some people were denying the reality of Christ's mission in this world and claimed that they were without sin (1:10). By this, they showed that they did not have a superior spirituality – they did not have God's Word in them at all.

So what are we to do when the light of God reveals more and more grime in the back corners of our inner life? We should remember God's plan for our sin – the death of Jesus on the cross (1:7). We should confess our sin so that he might continue to forgive and purify us (1:9) and we should rest not in our sin, nor in our push for perfection, but in God's perfect plan to deal with it (2:1,2).

> My dear children, I write this to you so that you will not sin. But if anybody does sin, we have an advocate with the Father – Jesus Christ the Righteous One.
>
> **1 John 2:1**

RESPOND

God does not condone any sin in our lives but he knows all about it. What's more, he has done everything to take care of it. Praise him for the wonder of the cross!

Bible in a year: Amos 7,8; Revelation 8

Living in the light of love

PREPARE

Does a dog bark to become a dog, or because it is one? Does a fish swim to become a fish? Do we become Christians by how we act? Or are our actions the result of who we are in Christ?

READ

1 John 2:3–11

EXPLORE

How can we know that we are in Christ? Verses 3 to 6 make it clear. The love of God enters a life, and the Word of God comes in. Subsequently, there is a response as the person grows in their likeness to the God with whom they are in a relationship. John is not saying that obedience leads to knowing God. He is saying that knowing God leads to obedience.

So, do we have a great list of commandments to remember and obey? No. Jesus made it simple. His followers are to love. Love God and love your neighbour. Just as Jesus taught his disciples at the Last Supper (John 13:34,35). Now, if someone claims to love God but hates his brother or sister, then they are not living in the light as they claim to be (v 9).

As we see in verse 11, the problem is that when someone is still walking around in the darkness, they are blind to that reality and don't know it.

> But if anyone obeys his word, love for God is truly made complete in them.
>
> **1 John 2:5**

RESPOND

Do you ever reverse 'I am loved, so I obey' into 'I obey in order to be loved'? Ask God to reassure your heart about his love for you. Pray for God's help to truly love your brothers and sisters in Christ.

Bible in a year: Amos 9; Revelation 9

You cannot love both

PREPARE

In a healthy marriage, whether in real life or a fairy tale, partners only have eyes for one another. Where have you observed that kind of faithful devotion or wished it were present?

READ

1 John 2:12–17

EXPLORE

Holiness is not simply about morality. Ultimately, holiness flows from our fellowship with God. So John addresses the believers as dear children whose sins are forgiven and who know God. The older believers he addresses as fathers who know the unchanging God. The younger believers he addresses as young men who overcome the evil one by the word of God living in them. Christianity is about a relationship with God worth fighting to enjoy.

A marriage involves genuinely loving someone and, therefore, not loving others in the same way. So John moves, in verses 15 to 17, to remind the believers that as lovers of God they must not love the world. As for Adam and Eve in the Garden of Eden, the world around continues to entice us away from devotion to God.

The lust of the flesh and the lust of the eyes draw us with sensory overload. The pride of life swells the vanity within to pull us away from him. We cannot love the world and still love God.

> Do not love the world or anything in the world. If anyone loves the world, love for the Father is not in them.
>
> **1 John 2:15**

RESPOND

Ask God to reveal if any part of your life reflects a love for the world instead of him. Thank God for his faithfulness to us. How reassuring to know that he wants us to have eyes for only him.

Bible in a year: Obadiah; Psalms 142,143

Real super Christianity

PREPARE

Consider for a moment why the enemy of God would want to bring tension and division to a local church. What damage can it do to the people of the church and the people of the area?

READ

1 John 2:18-27

EXPLORE

The history of the church is littered with disputes and divisions. Many whole denominations have resulted from church splits. It is clear why the enemy would like to multiply this kind of damage. However, it can be challenging to keep a clear perspective when you are in the middle of a local situation.

A group had left the church that John was writing to in this letter. They had not departed because of a personality clash or a preference for different worship music. They believed they had a superior spirituality and a higher grasp of truth. They denied the Trinity, rejected the Son and undermined the reality of eternal life itself (vs 20-23).

So John wrote to the remaining group to reassure them that they had the truth and the Spirit of God living in them (v 20). This anointing meant they did not need the 'super-spiritual' teaching of the group that had left. If there is a super-anything in Christianity, then it is the presence of the Holy Spirit whom every true believer in Jesus already has to help us abide in Christ (vs 24-27).

> No one who denies the Son has the Father; whoever acknowledges the Son has the Father also.
>
> **1 John 2:23**

RESPOND

Pray for God to protect your church from division. Pray for God to give every true believer in your church the assurance that comes from having his Spirit living in them!

Bible in a year: Jonah 1,2; Revelation 10

Wedding preparations

PREPARE

How does a bride prepare for her wedding? How would your life look different if you were convinced that Jesus could return and take you home to be with him, perhaps even today?

READ

1 John 2:28 – 3:10

EXPLORE

After using end-times language to speak of the enemy, John now looks forward with hope and anticipation. Jesus is coming again! And because we are now children of God, we can look forward confidently and without shame (2:29). Those who hope for this bridegroom will purify themselves in anticipation!

The group that John was writing to was being bombarded by criticism from the group that had left the church (see 2:18–26). They claimed to have a superior spirituality, but they were actually living with greater sinfulness. That context helps us understand what John writes in chapter 3, verses 4 to 10.

Christians do not achieve sinless perfection in this life, but the gospel makes a difference in our lives. While we may slip into sin (see 1:8; 2:1), our lives should not be characterised by persistent unchecked sin (3:6). The gospel is not just an external legal pardon for sin but also an internal, heart-transforming reality. The Spirit of God in us changes us from the inside out. So while Christians struggle with sin, we will not be defined by it. By God's Spirit, we have a new spiritual DNA.

> See what great love the Father has lavished on us, that we should be called children of God! And that is what we are!
>
> **1 John 3:1**

RESPOND

How has the Spirit working in you brought cleansing from sin? What areas of struggle is he still working on in you? Thank God for all he has done and will do in your life.

Bible in a year: Jonah 3,4; Revelation 11

1 John 3:11–24

Loving when unloved

PREPARE

Have you ever experienced unkindness from people who claim to be Christians? Why does it hurt so much more when it comes from those who are supposed to be family?

READ

1 John 3:11–24

EXPLORE

Now the theme shifts from God is light to God is love. In verse 11, John refers to the upper room where Jesus gave his command to love one another (John 13:34,35). Human nature in this fallen world is to hate one another, so if the world hates you, don't be surprised (vs 12–15). This was helpful clarification for these believers who were experiencing hateful attitudes from the group that had left – whose actions were not supporting their super-spiritual claims.

Christians do not have to guess what it means to love one another. We have the perfect example. Just as Jesus laid down his life for us, so we should practically, materially and sacrificially lay down what is ours for the sake of one another (vs 16–18).

How should we react if others hate us, even if they claim to be Christians? We should respond with Christlike love

(vs 16,18). And we can have the assurance of our standing before God because we believe in Jesus and have the Holy Spirit in us (vs 19–24).

> This is how we know what love is: Jesus Christ laid down his life for us. And we ought to lay down our lives for our brothers and sisters.
>
> **1 John 3:16**

RESPOND

Imagine what it was like for Jesus to go to the cross and lay down his life in love for us. Pray that he would stir his love in our hearts for one another, and show us practically what that looks like today.

Bible in a year: Micah 1–3; Psalm 144

Obeying God's Word

PREPARE

Think of someone, possibly someone you know, who has lived in obedience to God's Word through their lives. What does their life look like? How is it different from those who ignore God's Word?

- -

READ

Psalm 119:129–152

EXPLORE

In these three sections of Psalm 119, the writer continues to praise the wonders of God's Word (v 129). It gives light (v 130), it directs our steps (v 133), it is tried, tested and true (vs 140–142) and it provides understanding and delight (vs 143,144). And for the writer of this psalm, the bottom line is clear. God's Word is to be obeyed: 'Your statutes are wonderful; therefore I obey them' (v 129). He references obedience, directly or indirectly, at least seven times in these verses.

As well as celebrating God's good instruction and his desire to live in response to it, the psalmist also contemplates those who do not. He finds himself growing weary because of his zeal for God's Word when God's enemies ignore it (v 139). As he thinks of those who do *not* obey God's Word,

streams of tears flow from his eyes (v 136). If only they would long for God's Word as he does (v 131).

> Streams of tears flow from my eyes, for your law is not obeyed.
>
> Psalm 119:136

RESPOND

Take a moment to pray for people you know whose unresponsiveness to God's Word causes you distress. God did a miracle in your heart to stir a love for his instruction. Pray that he will do the same in theirs.

- -

Bible in a year: Micah 4,5; Revelation 12

97

True Spirit, true love

PREPARE

Suppose you had to devise a list of non-negotiable characteristics for a true group of Jesus' followers. What would be on that list? How should the church be distinct from every social group in modern society?

READ

1 John 4:1–12

EXPLORE

In yesterday's passage, John stated that Christianity involves believing in the Son and loving one another (3:23). He now deals with both aspects in more detail. Our assurance comes from the Spirit of God living in us, but there are other spirits in the world too. In chapter 4, verses 1 to 6, John tells the believers to test the spirits. The Holy Spirit will always celebrate the truth of who Jesus is – and the Holy Spirit is living in us and at work in us! False spirits undermine the truth of who Jesus is and what he has done (vs 2,3).

In verses 7 to 12, John addresses the issue of loving one another. This command is not just a pragmatic suggestion. Our love for one another reflects the great truth of who God is. True love comes from God himself (vs 7,8)! We do not have to look into ourselves and try to pump up some loving effort from within. No, the love comes from God to us – then it will flow from us to one another.

> You, dear children, are from God and have overcome them, because the one who is in you is greater than the one who is in the world.
>
> 1 John 4:4

RESPOND

How might false prophets be at work in your life to point you away from the truth and love of Jesus Christ (v 1)? How might the Holy Spirit want to stir your heart with the reality of Jesus' love today?

Bible in a year: Micah 6,7; Revelation 13

Heavenly love

PREPARE

Think of some human relationships that feel safe and secure to you. Thank God for them! Why are some relationships laced with fear?

READ

1 John 4:13–21

EXPLORE

Remember, John wrote to a group of true believers rocked by the departure of a group from their church. That other group spoke critically of them and celebrated their own supposedly superior spirituality. John wrote to reassure the faithful believers that they were not missing out on God's great work in the world. Their reassurance was that God had given them his Holy Spirit (v 13), which was evident because they loved one another (v 16).

As we saw yesterday, Christian love is not something we can work up in ourselves. It is a response to God first loving us (v 19). And genuine love for God and one another is such a miracle in this fallen world that it can give us a confidence that is beyond this world (v 17). Many relationships are tainted by fear, but there is an alternative (v 18). The miracle of Christian love is that it gives us the confidence to stand before God.

Why? Because this love is not about our efforts. It is the love of God at work in us. As the Spirit enables you to worship Christ, fellowship with God is the real deal (v 16).

> We love because he first loved us.
> 1 John 4:19

RESPOND

Ask God to fill you with his love so that it drives out any fear you feel about facing him one day. Pray that his miraculous, unconditional love will spill out from you to others today.

Bible in a year: Nahum 1–3; Revelation 14

Christianity needs Jesus

PREPARE

Could you live a 'Christian life' without Christ? Do you sometimes behave as though that were possible?

READ

1 John 5:1–12

EXPLORE

Some things just make sense for Christians (vs 1–5). Belief in Jesus is, of course, how we become Christians. Following on, it makes sense to love God and God's other children too. Because we love God, it makes sense to obey his commands. In fact, because of that love, God's commands do not feel like a burden. It is this inner transformation in a believer that ultimately brings victory over the antagonism of the world (v 4).

The false teachers behind the group leaving the church did not believe that Christ was genuinely human. Their belief system denied the reality of the incarnation. So John calls on three witnesses to Jesus being human. The water probably referred to his baptism, the blood referred to the crucifixion and the Spirit witnessed his entire mission on earth. God himself affirmed that the incarnation was true (vs 6–8; see also Matthew 3:17).

The bottom line, for John, is evident (vs 9–12). Either you accept the Father's testimony to the Son or you do not. You cannot have God the Father while dismissing the reality of the Son coming into this world to give us life.

Whoever has the Son has life; whoever does not have the Son of God does not have life.

1 John 5:12

RESPOND

Are there aspects of living the Christian life that you find tiring? Could you be trying to live obediently in your own strength? How can you find strength from drawing closer to God the Trinity?

Bible in a year: Habakkuk 1–3; Psalm 145